MW01260195

THE FREEDOM PROMISE

7 Steps to Stop Fearing What Food Will Do TO You
and Start Embracing What It Can Do FOR You

MINDY GORMAN-PLUTZER

BALBOA.
PRESS
A DIVISION OF HAY HOUSE

Balboa Press books may be ordered through booksellers or by contacting:

Balboa Press
A Division of Hay House
1663 Liberty Drive
Bloomington, IN 47403
www.balboapress.com
1 (877) 407-4847

Because of the dynamic nature of the Internet, any web addresses or links contained in this book may have changed since publication and may no longer be valid. The views expressed in this work are solely those of the author and do not necessarily reflect the views of the publisher, and the publisher hereby disclaims any responsibility for them.

The author of this book does not dispense medical advice or prescribe the use of any technique as a form of treatment for physical, emotional, or medical problems without the advice of a physician, either directly or indirectly. The intent of the author is only to offer information of a general nature to help you in your quest for emotional and spiritual well-being. In the event you use any of the information in this book for yourself, which is your constitutional right, the author and the publisher assume no responsibility for your actions.

Any people depicted in stock imagery provided by Thinkstock are models, and such images are being used for illustrative purposes only. Certain stock imagery © Thinkstock.

Printed in the United States of America.

ISBN: 978-1-4525-1954-8 (sc)
ISBN: 978-1-4525-1956-2 (hc)
ISBN: 978-1-4525-1955-5 (e)

Library of Congress Control Number: 2014913751

Balboa Press rev. date: 09/24/2014

For Ricki and Dani,

because of what was,
because of what is,
and for all that is still to come.

For Jill,

You lived everyday with grace and dignity. Your
enormous capacity for love and brilliant courage
will forever be a source of inspiration.

Freedom (noun) – adapted from Wikipedia

1: the power or right to act, speak, or think as one wants without hindrance or restraint:

    a) the state of not being imprisoned or restrained
    b) the state of being physically unrestricted and able to move easily
    c) (freedom from) the state of not being subject to or affected by a particular undesirable thing

2: the power of self-determination attributed to the will; the quality of being independent or fate or necessity

    "No one is free who is a slave to the body."—Lucious Annaeus Seneca

In the infinity of life where I am, all is perfect, whole and complete. I now choose to calmly and objectively see my old patterns and I am willing to make changes. I am teachable. I can learn. I am willing to change. I choose to have fun while doing this. I choose to react as though I have found a treasure when discovering something else to release. I see and feel myself changing moment by moment. Thoughts no longer have any power over me. I am the power in the world. I choose to be free. All is well in my world.

—Louise Hay, *You Can Heal Your Life*

CONTENTS

INTRODUCTION

Laying the Foundation, Framing the Steps, Celebrating Lasting Freedom

It recently dawned on me that I have spent most my adult life either trying to put weight on or take weight off. Taking time to relish where I was never occurred to me. I look back on holidays, birthdays, shopping excursions, school trips, and vacations and remember the energy I spent thinking about my weight, how I perceived my body to look, what I was going to eat, and how I would handle food in its abundance or scarcity.

I will never have that time back, those minutes, hours, and days. I won't remember things my daughters told me during those times or the experiences I had with friends and loved ones.

My story is the motivation behind and inspiration for *The Freedom Promise*, my private coaching practice where I help clients free themselves from the challenges and disordered eating behaviors brought on by their toxic relationships with food. My experience confirms that while what we eat is important to our health, well-being, and waistlines, the extra weight so many carry around is merely a symptom, the body's way of calling attention to the fact that something needs to be looked at. It may be stress-related, or clutter that needs clearing, or even an undigested issue that needs to be let go of.

Instead of attacking ourselves for carrying the extra weight, I am sharing the supportive steps that have helped me and hundreds of my clients to embrace it, accept it, and relax into the process of letting it go, at the same time offering helpful and proven techniques to deliver you to a place of peace and serenity.

I am willing to make a safe assumption that you know how to diet—how to cut calories, fats, and carbs in an effort to manage your weight, presumably to lose some of it. I think it is fair for me to think that you are up-to-date on all the latest nutritional theories— what's in and what's out.

I also think it's likely that while you know how to diet, you are often confused about how to eat. Perhaps any pleasure you get from food is accompanied by a hearty dose of guilt and you are longing for joy and spontaneity from your relationship with food.

This book is not intended to be another diet book, although there is a good possibility that if you follow my steps and adopt the strategies I lay out, you will release extra weight as you release the hold food has on you. This book is also not designed to diagnose or cure any psychological issues you feel may have contributed to your toxic relationship with food. What this book is designed for is to help you reclaim the power that has been taken from you by a $60 billion diet industry intent on filling you with falsehoods so you believe you aren't capable of discerning or trusting what is nourishing for you.

My intention in writing this book is to help you navigate the confusion surrounding what to eat so you can finally stop fearing what food will do *to* you and embrace the nourishing wisdom, the beauty and intelligence of what food can do *for* you.

This book will be valuable to you if

- you are sick and tired of getting on and off the diet roller coaster;
- your mood is determined by a number on the scale each morning (or throughout the day);
- eating less and exercising more isn't working for you;
- you can't stand the thought of deprivation;

- you are confused by all of the nutritional information in the news;
- you begin every morning vowing to "be good" and end the day vowing to start again tomorrow;
- you feel challenged by life-cycle changes and turn to food for comfort;
- you are facing the struggles that come with recovery and would benefit from support; or
- you are ready to stop blaming your lack of willpower and instead empower yourself to stop dieting and start living.

What you will learn is that *how*, *why*, and *when* we eat has an impact on *what* we eat. You will learn to make empowered choices from the sacred space within you that is grateful, accepting, and forgiving. You will learn about honoring your appetite, for appetite is life, and how stressing over your desire to have the body of your dreams will work to sabotage your efforts. You will find relief in knowing that punishing exercise is not necessary and discover ways to move that honor your body rather than make it go away. You will discover how food is so much more than calories and develop a respect for the colorful and intricate beauty of it. And lastly, I will ask you to look at how you can be nourished in ways that have nothing to do with food.

Sprinkled throughout each chapter are stories about my own disordered and toxic relationship with food. I share the craziness of almost half a century being tied to irrational beliefs and ridiculous behaviors with food and exercise. I offer my philosophy for living the big, beautiful, and truly nourished life I have today and in many cases, back it up with science. I suggest action you can take so you can finally experience the *freedom* you long for. If you want to take it further, I have included recommended reading from some of the foremost respected teachers and leaders in the fields of wellness, nutrition, and spirituality.

I hope you will come away enlightened and motivated to reinvent your relationship with food and your body from one that is rooted in fear and confusion to one that offers you true and lasting nourishment. If how we do one thing is how we do everything, this newly nourished version of self can only emerge as brilliant and amazing. I want you to know that being truly nourished allows you to have an expanded presence rather than the diminished one that lurks when we spend our energies trying to be smaller.

For me, a diminished existence meant I kept myself small by fearing who I would be if I wasn't the perfect wife, mother, sister, daughter, and friend. A big part of that picture was tied to outward beauty, and for me that meant I had to be thin, very thin. The pursuit of perfection does crazy things to us. It distorts reality and ends up actually being the pursuit of failure. For years I wore my perfectionism like a badge of honor. Eventually, the weight of it became an unbearable burden. Letting go of it allowed me to experience a lightness of being that is so much more desirable and sustainable. It's actually euphoric and sometimes makes me giddy.

Every one of us has a story, and each of our stories differ. Very often it is the attachment to that story that needs to be let go of.

This book contains many calls for letting go—letting go of toxic thoughts, clutter, outdated science, and habits that no longer serve us. While I know firsthand that letting go is a difficult and challenging thing to do, holding on only serves to hold us back and prevent us from realizing our full potential; for what we resist, persists. I ask you to trust that with letting go you make room for growth that can set you free in a way that allows you to have the life you are now only imagining.

My history with dieting and wanting a body other than the one I had started early, in my early teens. Always a rail-thin child, I rounded out during puberty. Restricting calories was a way of life in my family's home, and ever the obedient daughter, I came onboard and made it my mission to do it well. I received mixed messages, though.

I remember the days my mother went grocery shopping. She would take hours filling up three wagons of food and then putting it away—cleaning the chickens before she froze them, piling the pastry boxes on the counter, filling the cookie jar, and standing the cans of vegetables on top of one another, just so, in the cabinet.

Breakfasts that I remember were sugar-coated flakes or toaster pastries. On weekends we had bagels and an array of spreads and smoked fish. Dinners were healthy according to the standards of the '50s and '60s—lots of red meat. I recall occasional chicken, covered in cornflake crumbs or sweet sauces, meatloaf, and lamb chops. On weekends we ate frozen meals as my parents dined out. Sunday dinner was usually Chinese food—including wonton soup, egg rolls, spare ribs, and fried rice. I assure you there was no steamed chicken and broccoli.

Weekdays were all about eating as little as we could during the day, but once Friday came, it was a food fest. I remember little talk about nutrition, more about food being good or bad. Looking back, I never gave any thought to it, I just went along. So began the confusion and belief that good food was about safe calories, bad food causes weight gain, weight gain makes you fat, and fat is undesirable.

I remember all the crazy diets we tried; The Stillman diet, where we drank a lot of water and ate a lot of meat; The Cabbage Soup Diet, when we'd go through huge pots of soup that was loaded with gaseous vegetables and instant onion soup mix. Then there were the forays into Atkins, Pritikin, and Diet Center. We never went clothes shopping without "trying to lose a few pounds," so I never felt I was okay the way I was.

The vicious cycle of overeating and restricting had begun. Soon I discovered the appetite suppressants, diuretics, and laxatives in my mother's bathroom cabinet. The scale became the magic mirror that answered my question about being good enough. I judged my self-worth and value by the size of my thighs, but my mind's eye was tainted by the feedback from the scale. I had lost the ability to see myself for who I was. I had no connection to my body.

College life in the 1970s introduced me to other ways of controlling my appetite—diet pills I had been prescribed so I could pull all-nighters studying and the recreational cocaine that my peers and I believed wasn't addictive. Some days I would consume nothing but Tab (the popular diet soft drink of the time) and Light n' Lively ice milk, some concoction of nonfat dairy and artificial sweeteners that mimicked ice cream. I had also discovered alcohol and late night "munchies," so my weight continued to be all over the place.

During my last year in college, I met Stuart, who became my husband a short time later. We settled on Long Island, not far from where we grew up, and the fairy-tale life I was groomed for began. Before long I was pregnant with our first daughter. Determined not to carry any extra baby weight, I continued to be excessive in my calorie counting and managed to gain just twenty pounds. Fifteen months later, pregnant again, becoming more obsessed with my ill-perceived body image, I kept my weight gain to just seventeen pounds and was so proud that I had delivered another healthy daughter weighing more than seven pounds. I spent my twenties going through the motions of growing up but never truly doing so.

By the time I was in my midthirties, I was consumed with being the thinnest person in the room. I can remember stepping on the bathroom scale many times a day—after every meal, after every bathroom visit, undressed and dressed. Stuart and I were living a blessed life with our two daughters, who were growing up to be exceptional young women. We joined the local country club, became active in various community causes, and had wonderful friends. All that was missing was me. I was unable to feel comfortable in my own skin. I would panic over dinner plans with friends but secretly eat a jar of peanuts before dinner. I would measure six ounces of wine to have with dinner at home but order three glasses of wine while dining out, and I would pick on sugar cubes from the bowl when coffee was served.

I had trouble balancing a monthly budget, but if you asked me how many calories I consumed at any given meal, I could answer without hesitation. As numerically challenged as I am, I was a brilliant number cruncher when it came to my diet.

It was insanity.

Soon I realized I needed help to break out of this destructive pattern. I sought help from my internist, who referred me to a therapist and a nutritionist. My routine included weekly weigh-ins, meal plans, and two to three visits a week to the therapist. The internist prescribed antidepressants and Xanax, the therapist blamed my mother and my husband, and the nutritionist wanted me eating tuna-salad sandwiches, ice cream shakes in the afternoon, and lasagna for dinner washed down with two glasses of wine. I was terrified. What I decided I really needed was an exorcist.

Meanwhile, as I was getting smaller, my daughters were gaining weight, making clear they didn't want to be like me. We were in a fine mess. I describe that time as feeling as if I were in a black hole; a sewer with the manhole cover askew so that I could see the light, my way out, but was unable to pull myself up and out.

Insane and out of control as I was, I had the sense not to start my girls on the diet roller-coaster nightmare. We all had healing to do, and from somewhere deep within me I knew the work was about self-acceptance, self-care, and letting go of needing to be a better version of what I perceived myself to be. I watched my words, studied and worked on my own nutrition, becoming very aware of how my behavior with and fear of food was impacting my children.

Many years later, my daughter had finished reading The Hunger Games, a 2008 sci-fi bestseller. When she mentioned this, my son-in-law quipped that he thought she was referring to how life was growing up in our home. We were all able to laugh.

It took time and working through issues that were unique to me, but I eventually found a connection between eating wholesome, nutritious food and a newfound energy level. I was able to concentrate, and my fears about getting fat were diminishing.

At this time, in 1995, I went to work for a local nutritional counseling center. The owner believed in me, my recovery, and hired me to see clients. This was irony at its best. I was actually being sought out and paid to share the weight-loss secrets that had me by a chokehold for more years than I care to remember. I continued to practice this nutritional counseling for the following seven years, at the center and then on my own, but deep down I felt like a fraud.

In the years that followed, my midforties, life couldn't have been better. It appeared my family and I had it all. I was still careful to watch what I ate, but my severe restricting was a thing of the past, my overeating was infrequent, and I felt healthy and in control. In December of 2002, all that changed when Stuart was diagnosed with stage IV malignant melanoma. There was no proven protocol, no drug to give us any chance for a cure. Our only hope was a clinical trial, but none proved to be successful. Eighteen months later we knew we had come to the end. There was nothing more to do but accept and adjust. Two coping mechanisms I hadn't mastered.

Hospice was a part of our home life now. My role as caregiver defined my days and nights. I started to drink heavily—no longer the fun social drinking that was a big part of our lives. I waited until five p.m. to start, until I was starting at four. Eventually, I found myself taking swigs from the ever-present open bottle. Alcohol had become the extension of my disordered eating and could have easily been a jar of peanuts, a cheesecake, or a pint of ice cream.

We lost Stuart in August, 2004. The aftermath of losing your husband is so very multifaceted. At first it was a relief of sorts because his suffering was over. Then you try to find your life again. You never do—not the life you had before. My family and friends showered me with heartfelt devotion. I was surrounded by love, but wine became my lover, and remained so for some time to come.

Here I was, forty-nine years old, a single mother, responsible for handling finances and finding a new purpose for my life. I was in serious trouble, again. I didn't know how to be alone.

Again, I knew I needed help. The stakes had gotten too high. An eating disorder is a private hell. You can fool people into thinking all is wonderful—that you are just a perfect dieter. If you are too thin, they either admire or admonish you. Compulsive eating shows up as having pounds to lose. But alcohol abuse extends to family and friends and drags them into your hell. In my case, I was sloppy, slurred my words, and couldn't walk out of a restaurant without fear of falling. I forgot phone calls and had too many embarrassing moments. My life became all about me—I was the victim. A victim of dysfunction, victim of a life interrupted, victim of the tools I could use to numb me from the pain and sorrow.

Finally I was done being sick and tired. I now had a grandson, and I was determined to be an ever-present part of his life. I took some bold steps toward really looking at my addictive behaviors and discovered they were coming from the same place—the fear-based lies I told myself about not being enough and the inability to face my feelings. That negative self-talk was nothing more than a scary bedtime story. I woke up to the fact that there is no such thing as the Big Bad Wolf or Wicked Witch, analogies for the lies I told myself about the feelings I feared feeling, of not being good enough. I discovered that my foray into alcohol abuse occurred because I hadn't addressed the issues driving my behaviors and beliefs about food and my body.

I went back to work counseling people, but not until I had become a board-certified health coach. I no longer share secrets about how lose weight but share my truth about letting go of the undigested burdens that are weighing us down and not letting our light emerge.

While my story starts with food and the desire for perfection, it's really about recovery—in the literal sense of regaining what was lost or stolen. It's about finding *freedom* from the bondage of self, no matter what your compulsion.

I share my story to help you understand that I know what it means to be disconnected from your body. I know how life can present situations where we need to reinvent our very existence.

You may be wondering what changed for me and when it all came together. While I can tell you the date of my last drink, my recovery from disordered eating wasn't marked by a line in the sand. It more resembled a cloud lifting gradually. As I educated myself about the true meaning of nutrition and nourishment, I practiced embodiment as I learned to love movement. Moving rather than punishing exercise allowed me to connect to the healthy parts of myself that were strong and flexible. I explored my relationship to fear-based living and discovered the practice of integrity to self. I doubt any of this would have resonated and remained with me had I not found incredible support from friends and professionals alike who continue to guide and mentor me.

One day I realized I had forgotten to weigh myself. Another day, I ran out of the house without giving thought to how my thighs looked in my pants. Days that followed brought excitement, rather than anxious anticipation, about going to a new restaurant. Many days I forgot to ask for my salad dressing on the side and actually finished my salad as it was served to me. I started filling candy bowls without fearing their presence in my home would trigger a binge.

I allowed myself to experience uncomfortable feelings and situations. I learned that no feeling is more uncomfortable than the discomfort I feel by *not* facing it. I had to acknowledge my insecurities and fears for what they were—False Evidence Appearing Real. I could let go of having to be perfect and adopt the belief that nothing is—perfection is just a perception that is not rooted in reality. I started to fully understand what it means to be connected to my body, to feel present and alive. Being connected to my body allows me to honor my appetite and satisfy what I am hungry for.

Feeling present allows me to be an active participant in my life, and I no longer want to walk through it in an alcohol- or food-induced haze. I fell in love again—with me. I discovered I am great company. I don't have to consume myself with obsessive behaviors in an effort to keep busy.

As I started to look at food differently, I stopped fearing the calories, fat, and carbohydrates. I learned that calories are energy, and that my body needs protein, fat, and carbohydrates to survive. I can make empowered choices about the types of proteins, fats, carbs, and calories I put in my body, and yes, I can eat a lot of great quality food and maintain the healthy weight I feel good about. As I am empowered, I trust myself with food, appreciating and accepting its complexity. Hunger is no longer a source of anxiety. I no longer hide behind my body and a warped perception of it. I eat what I want, when I want, and trust that I will stop when I have had enough. I engage in exercise that I enjoy and will skip a workout when tired. I choose to surround myself with the people, places, and things that remind me what my life is about and allow me to fulfill my desires and life's purpose.

Today, I am lucky and so very happy to have found love again with a new husband who nurtures my desire for continued growth. Life is full as we are each blessed with amazing children, fabulous in-law children, and spectacular grandchildren.

I still find myself looking for something to eat if I am bored and sometimes leave the table having eaten too much. There are times my ears perk up over talk of the latest diet and I get tempted to buy in to one of the many cleanses offered in my inbox. I don't always feel great in or about my aging body. I have days when I feel sad and want to isolate. I still grieve the past, but I, more often and with more intensity, rejoice and celebrate the present. I respect the darkness and embrace the light. I have connected with my deepest sense of self, which for me translates to my highest self, my higher power. I sometimes need to remind myself to let go of the expectations that may disappoint. The difference now is that I have awareness for what I know needs to keep happening for me to stay where I am and where I want to be.

My heartfelt desire is that by sharing this part of myself, along with the guidelines I have lain out for you in the coming pages, you will find peace in both the darkness and the light.

May you emerge from the shadows to believe completely in yourself, because you are complete, just the way you are. Get comfortable, cozy up, and join me as I lead you through the seven steps to food freedom.

CHAPTER 1

Find Your Enough, Face Your Feelings, Feel the Love

"What happens in your mind determines your experience of life."
—Marianne Williamson

Let me take you back to how my days began. Upon awakening, I would immediately run my hands over my stomach to feel how concave or round it was. I needed to feel my hipbones. Getting out of bed and making my way to the scale was exhilarating. I liked playing a game with myself where I would guess my weight before stepping on. A good number invigorated me and actually made me feel high. Insanely, a number that was more than my desired weight served its purpose as well. It meant I would have to restrict, and there was great comfort and safety in that as well. It had become routine for me to step on and off three times, checking the accuracy of the scale, questioning its position on the tile floor. I had given up my power to the scale, defining myself by what I imagined others saw about me from the outside. I lived according to thoughts created by the inner voice that told me I needed to "be" thinner, smarter, or more of something.

For a long time, I believed I was broken. It didn't matter that I was in a loving marriage, had raised two daughters who were kind, generous of spirit, and highly successful in their respective lives. I couldn't shake the negative self-talk that came from believing I wasn't enough or that there were circumstances in my life that I judged to be unfair.

Not until I accepted recovery in the sense of regaining what was lost or taken, was I even aware of how much of a choice I have regarding how I react to what life hands me. I've come to view life as a poker game—I can pick up the cards dealt me, hold them in hopes of a winning hand, or I can fold, confident in the knowledge that this round has reached its rightful end and there will be other chances to play.

Focusing on what I am grateful for required a shift in my mindset and a new way of being. I started with simple gratitude for my realization that I needed to be grateful. Next came gratitude for the journey itself and my commitment to it, even though the journey was difficult at times.

What followed were monumental shifts in my thinking as I opened up to the possibility of being enveloped by the love in my life. I developed a willingness to ask for the peace and serenity I longed for. I started to notice the beauty of the world around me—for example, cloud formations and the colors of the sky at sunset. My mind got quiet, and I could relax into the paradox that even with all the uncertainty, life was as it was supposed to be. Soon, the things I was grateful for were around me in abundance as I released the negativity that held me back.

When we disengage from the inner voice of negativity and realize it is not telling the truth, we are no longer boxed into our thoughts and we can fully inhabit our bodies. This experience can be spiritual in nature as a kind of magic occurs when we tap into the wonder and natural beauty of the body we possess.

When we do this, we change in that we operate from a place of love rather than fear—the fear of not being "enough." Love allows us to be forgiving and compassionate. When we are present like this, love starts with ourselves. We can live in gratitude, focusing on what we have rather than what we think is missing, opening us up to the possibilities that we can handle whatever comes our way.

While this first step is the foundation for your journey to food freedom, it is also the ultimate goal. I am not asking you to render yourself powerless; rather, I am guiding you to empower yourself as you disengage from fear and limiting beliefs that keep you repeating compulsive and unhealthy behaviors.

Willpower doesn't work, as it implies an all-or-nothing control exerted to restrain us from self-indulgence. Willingness is a kinder state of being that prepares us to accept change from a loving place, a more feminine approach that is more aligned with the journey. When the journey includes self-kindness and connecting to the truth buried in our souls, we reclaim what we've forgotten as we lost ourselves in food and negative thoughts about our bodies.

As I hope you discover in this chapter and in the following pages, your relationship with food is a reflection of your relationship to yourself and your story. Our stories differ from one another but nonetheless they got us to the same place of fear and uncertainty.

Maybe you feel you need to handle everything by yourself; maybe you have larger-than-life issues that create the sense of you having to be bigger to carry all those issues; maybe when things start to go well you don't think you deserve it; maybe you are afraid of losing a loved one if you look or act a certain way. The reason doesn't matter. What matters is that your desire to change your relationship with food is not about becoming more or less of yourself, but becoming more authentic to yourself.

When you lovingly transform your relationship to yourself, you transform your relationship to everything else.

It starts with gratitude. Gratitude awakens us to being open and connected to our selves and others like nothing else. It allows us to stay in the present moment and even accept our flaws and imperfections, enabling us to feel at ease, a lightness of being that will bring us home to ourselves.

Practicing gratitude negates the two root causes of the disease of not enough. The first is a sense of dissatisfaction, which opens the door to the second: being consumed with and compulsive about trying to get more, be more, and be better in order to be happy and content. We think, "If only I could lose this weight; "If only I could get to the gym every day"; If only I can get my partner to communicate better"; "If only I had more money, a better job ..."

The gift of gratitude is that it reverses the pattern of looking outside ourselves and immediately puts us in touch with the many gifts and blessings already present in our lives. Gratitude allows us to be connected to the positive life force of *now*. Instead of waiting to lose the ten, fifteen, or thirty pounds in order to be happy, gratitude for the journey will bring happiness where you are so you can wear the great clothes today or have the talk now with your boss about the raise you deserve.

Gratitude helps to eradicate fear, unveiling the loving-kindness we need to live the fully nourished life we deserve and desire. Gratitude is a profoundly transformative practice and a big part of many cultures. In the Jewish spiritual tradition, for example, the very first words of prayer spoken upon wakening express gratitude for the gift of another day of life: "I am grateful. Thank you for returning my soul to me with great compassion." The Buddhist practice, too, is to begin each day with appreciation for the rare gift of a precious human birth and to contemplate its changing nature. One reflects: "How then shall I live this precious day?" and "What is important for me to recognize, remember, and pay attention to today?"

Even science has its theories about being grateful. Scientists have conducted research on gratitude and determined it to be an attitude, a mood, and an emotion.

Numerous studies support the profound effects of gratitude on the people who feel it. In one, subjects asked to complete weekly gratitude journals reported increased overall well-being as they exercised more, slept less fitfully, enjoyed better health, and had a more optimistic view of life.(1)

Even a one-time show of thoughtful gratitude will produce an immediate increase in happiness and decrease in depressive symptoms. Participants who kept up with their gratitude practice experienced long-lasting and positive results.(2)

Finding Your Enough

A heart filled with gratitude generates actions that complete the circle between the gifts offered, our willingness to receive, and the universal source of the gift.

Stepping into the sacred space of gratitude allows us to find our way back to the time we were comfortable—before our limiting beliefs took over and our story became one of needing to rely on compulsive behaviors in order to find that place again. The freshly baked brownie, the bag of chips, the glass of wine, or new pair of shoes will never satisfy if we aren't coming from a place of compassion and consciousness for the abundance we are surrounded with already.

Gratitude will bring you back to yourself, home to yourself, not to the image of who you think you should be. It allows you to move from "I am not" to "I am." Having said this, there is nothing wrong with wanting to be stronger, leaner, healthier, except when the quest becomes the bane of our existence, causing us to miss out on believing we are enough as we are. If you shame and deprive yourself into reaching a goal, any goal, you will reach it as a shamed and deprived person. When the journey is guided by positive energy, you arrive at the destination with vibrancy.

For many of us, believing in and finding our "enough" is challenging. We have forgotten our true nature—the essence of our authentic selves; the person we were before we let compulsive behaviors protect us from feelings we feared would derail us. We lost track of who we are because we came to believe that we are our thoughts, beliefs, feelings, and stories. We became separate from our bodies, rendering us homeless.

Gratitude focuses on what we already are and what we already have. Feeling gratitude turns our attention to the deeper sense of ourselves where we can believe we are enough and feel fulfillment. People who live grateful lives understand that pouring our best into the life we have now is the best reward, giving us the self-assurance and confidence to take us through the inevitable hard times.

When we connect with the part of ourselves that accepts who we are now, we begin to feel whole. We can add the joy, sorrow, success, and disappointment to the circle that completes us.

Face Your Feelings

Becoming aware and curious will allow you to question those deeply held beliefs and your reactions to scenarios that trigger you and question if these reactions are how you have to respond. Without awareness, we flounder and drift through life. With curiosity, we gain clarity and direction. Questioning our thoughts and beliefs opens us up to noticing them and finding out where they came from. The beautiful gift from this is the opportunity to be with ourselves.

When we face our feelings, we step into a place we never knew existed. We brilliantly turned to compulsive behaviors in an effort to numb us to those feelings we chose to avoid, even feared. Discovering that we can examine and question them, we learn they are not rooted in truth and that they need not be feared.

Question where the stories began. Were they the response to someone else's wounding? Can you find compassion for the origin of the story? Many of my generation were often told to "Stop crying or I'll give you a reason to cry." Maybe you heard, "Do as I say, not as I do." These messages told us we shouldn't feel, that we had to toughen up and stand strong. Chances are, the person who gave you that message was handed the same one. Once we become aware of the meaning behind the message, and follow through with questioning, we start to see that perhaps the story we are attached to is no longer working for us.

Accepting what we can't change and facing what we can makes room for forgiveness and huge personal growth. In that growth we begin to experience loving-kindness and compassion. Compassion leads to forgiveness and an end to struggling with what was. Forgiveness helps us to let go of judgment, anger, and ultimately fear. When we are forgiving and compassionate, we can find nourishment from within.

Best-selling author Melody Beattie teaches that if we identify the problem and feel the feelings, we can redirect the course of our lives. Be grateful for all of it—the blessing comes in being able to develop the awareness, feel the feelings, be humbled by this newfound gift, and then let it go if they no longer serves us.

Emotions become feelings, which become thoughts, which morph into beliefs. We lose ourselves to those beliefs in the sense that they take on a power of their own as they dictate who we think we are supposed to be. When we realize that feelings are only feelings and thoughts are only thoughts, not who we are, we can meet them and engage them.

Not feeling our feelings causes us to check out, making us numb and cut off from not only our feelings but from what is actually good and blessed in our lives. Once we face the feeling, meet it, and embrace it, we can gain confidence that our feeling no longer has that power over us.

Most of our beliefs are rooted in fear. The word *afraid* comes from the root word *frai*, which means "beloved, precious, at peace." When we add the prefix *A*, which means "away from," the word *afraid* means "being away from the state of feeling beloved, precious, and at peace." Fear wreaks havoc. It puts us into stress physiology and disconnects us from interacting with the wisdom of our bodies. When fear causes us to rely on strategies for survival, on a natural level it is a good thing as it is intended to protect us. Often, however, what we fear is not actually a threat and our fear is nothing more than an emotion we've invented.

All the promises to self and loved ones will continue to meet resistance until we can let go of our attachment to false and limiting beliefs about ourselves and the food we eat, or don't. The burden created in our minds shows up as excess baggage that eventually wears us down.

Letting go allows us to feel lighter. When we feel lighter, we become lighter. When you are *free*, you are able to make changes from the inside out, making it possible to change the outside as well.

Too much or too little food, too much or too little exercise is not the cause of our weight issues. Fear is often the cause, and that fear blocks our minds and hearts from love. Fear translates to confusion, and it can ebb and flow within us like the tide. It resides all around us, and if you are reading this book, then chances are it lives in your kitchen.

Let it know it is no longer welcome. Exorcise the demon of fear by finding the room within your self that you can return to safely. Create the space within you to welcome love so fully that there is no room for the fear. From that love we can access the inner wisdom we need to find compassion for ourselves.

Feel the Love

> We cultivate love when we allow our most vulnerable and powerful selves to be deeply seen and known, and when we honor the spiritual connection that grows from the offering with trust, respect, kindness and affection.
>
> —Brenee Brown

Love is an incredibly powerful force. We are all ultimately seeking it, in one form or another. If we are to be successful in finding that love, we must give it to ourselves first. Many of us have difficulty with this concept as we may not feel worthy or we may be harboring long-held beliefs from our pasts that insist we are not. To add love to the mix of feelings is to give our selves the experience of freeing our selves from the fear, to experience peace and all that is precious.

Falling in love with ourselves asks us to stop beating ourselves up and become willing to accept that we are human. In that humanness, we have had many different relationships with ourselves. We have had times when we liked ourselves more and times we've been disappointed in ourselves. It doesn't matter what our past story is;

adopting loving acceptance means we learn to accept ourselves for who we are, as well as who we are not.

As we envision a more loving relationship with ourselves, it is important that we look to parts of our story that we express compassion for. Feel love for the awkward and confused teen. Appreciate the scared you who perhaps alienated a loved one. Loving acceptance is also about learning to love and accept others as they are, as well as who they aren't and always do our best to respond with love and compassion. Compassion allows us to see with the eyes of wholeness.

Even when we experience a dark night of the soul, being aware of and able to tap in to loving-kindness means we possess the power to choose love over fear. Life then takes on a new dimension.

I am not referring to love in the romantic sense, rather a love that fills us with simple joy and serenity. The kind of love that once experienced, connects us to the part of ourselves that needs no distraction. We can stop thinking about how thin we want to be and discover a basic sense of being, without judgment. We can finally come home to ourselves with a full heart.

Nine years into my journey home to myself, I can feel the welcome mat beneath my feet, as I am finally grounded.

Hand in hand, my husband and I were strolling the stretch of beach that we call home. The sky was robin's-egg blue, the water at our feet not too cold, and the wind gentle enough to feel like a warm hug. The awareness of those moments created heartfelt joy as I experienced something new—being in love with me. Not a thought about my thighs or belly as I strolled the beach in my bathing suit, not a thought to what I had eaten that day or what dinner was going to look like. Not a judgment about the younger bodies on the beach. Making footprints in the sand was all I needed in that stretch of time to make me feel whole and complete.

Finding our enough, facing the feelings, and feeling the love allows for the realization that we are here and ready to shine like the brightest and most brilliant sun through all the highs and lows life presents, allowing us to return home with the brightest and most brilliant version of ourselves.

Embrace It

Gratitude Journal

- Begin each day with a silent or written **gratitude list**. Acknowledge five things you are grateful for. Pay attention to what surrounds you, the love and abundance, not what you wish was different. You are coming from the place of love, and you are open to receive the energy of the universe.

Define Where You Shine

- Name it and make it part of who you are. Ask what unique character traits you possess. Find your sense of humor, your wit and intelligence. Believe that these traits reflect the truth of who you are.

Reframe the Journey as "Progress at Play" rather than "a Work in Progress"

- Rather than having the mindset that it's going to take a lot of work for transformation to occur, have a more loving perspective and bring a joyful awareness to the positive that is unfolding in your life.

Be Mindful

- Focus on the present, not the past or future. This helps you to be aware of your surroundings and feelings.

Journal It

What do I need to let go of in order to taste the abundance in my life and appreciate who and where I am now?

_____

_____

_____

_____

_____

_____

_____

_____

_____

_____

_____

_____

_____

_____

Affirm It

Today I will be open to the concept of change. I will trust that the place where I'll be dropped off is better than the place where I was picked up. I know that change is necessary to take me wherever I need to go.

Today I will practice gratitude. I will get in the habit of saying thank you, even for the "problems" in my life, because these challenges are valuable lessons I can learn from. I will be grateful for the gift of gratitude.

Today I will ask for help to let go of my need to be afraid. I welcome peace, trust, acceptance, and safety into my life. I will make a point of listening to my healthy, rational fears and will relinquish all the others.

Today I will work at loving myself unconditionally. I will begin to let go of self-loathing and other unproductive behaviors. Today I want to hold myself in high self-esteem. I know I can do so.

Today I will begin to take healthy risks. I will ask the universe for assistance in letting go of my fear of failure ... and success. I will ask for help in fully living my life so that I can start experiencing all the wonderful parts of my journey.

Read More about It

Mary O'Malley, *The Gift of our Compulsions,* California, New World Library, 2004

Geneen Roth, *Women, Food and God,* New York, Scribner, 2010

Byron Katie and Steven Mitchell, *Loving What is*, New York, Three Rivers press, 2002

Hale Dwoskin and Jack Canfield, *The Sedona Method*: Your key to Lasting Happiness, Success, Peace and Emotional Well-Being, Sedona, Sedona Press, 2007

CHAPTER 2

Relax: The Weighty Issue of Stress

Most nights, I dedicated hours reviewing what I had eaten that day, meticulously and repeatedly calculating the calories and amounts of fat, carbohydrates, and protein. I would follow up by methodically planning what I would eat the following day. If we had social commitments, I would suffer serious anxiety beforehand, so fearful and stressed over the possibility of not having control over my food intake and what that would do to me. To undo the imagined threat my body suffered, I ended each evening with a handful of laxatives, my way of purging what I had consumed in the way of food and drink.

Even though my food choices were usually measured, I calmed my anxiety with several glasses of wine. As my sense of judgment got out of control, so did my perception of what I had eaten. Regardless, I needed to start each day with a clean slate. Some nights, I was so overcome because of the laxative abuse that I was sure I wasn't going to wake up the next day. I experienced cold sweats and heart palpitations because my stressed body was begging me to stop the madness. I made a few secret pacts with my God—if he would allow me to wake up the next day, I would stop the insanity of my behavior.

Mornings were hell. I felt as though I was hung over until I got to the scale for the validation I needed to feel redeemed.

One night in particular, my family and I went to dinner to celebrate my daughter's birthday. This restaurant was known for two things: "tiny 'tinis" and their signature dessert, "make your own s'mores." After several 'tinis, and a dinner I barely remember, the fixings for the s'mores were placed in the middle of the table. As our group assembled their graham crackers, chocolate bars, and marshmallows, I switched my chocolate for bars of ex-lax I had in my bag. There was no pleasure in the dessert for me; while everyone at the table was delighting over their creations, I was plotting and calculating the perceived damage of my meal and how to get rid of it.

It's hard to say what came first—stress about what food was going to do to me or stress over what I was doing to my body and the shame I felt about myself as a result of my behavior. I claimed food poisoning through the night and lost another opportunity for a positively memorable family evening.

If you are reading this book, there is a good chance that fears about food and weight dominate your thoughts. Negative body image and an unhealthy relationship with food can cause stress, but it works the other way around as well.

The relationship between stress and disordered eating is, in many ways, a vicious cycle: Feelings of being stressed or overwhelmed can trigger disordered eating behaviors, such as binge eating or restricting calories, which are used as a coping mechanism. And, in turn, the compulsive behavior, fears, and constant negative thoughts that characterize eating disorders raise stress levels.

Those who restrict often get a feeling of control. Unfortunately, what we control ends up controlling us. Those who binge oftentimes have a feeling of sedation and comfort. Not only do these compulsive behaviors with food cause the obvious physical stress to the body, they can exacerbate psychological stress.

Worrying about food and weight can be a source of considerable anxiety, leading to feelings of low self-esteem that elevate stress levels.

The Science of Stress

Stress is defined as any *real or imagined threat* and the body's response to that threat. Stress chemistry is powerful. It is biological wiring throughout the nervous system that enervates every nerve and every organ and reaches every cell. It is an evolutionary mechanism, as we are designed to run from perceived danger; an adaptation that evolved as our ancestors were chased by predatory creatures.

While there are no such creatures around today, our daily- and life-cycle issues weigh us down in a way that has us operating in survival mode. We can internalize financial worries, frustrations in our relationships, career pressures, and undigested burdens from the past.

When we are put in situations that cause us stress, blood rushes to our arms, legs, and every cell in our bodies; heart rate and blood pressure increases; our bodies release hormones such as cortisol and insulin, designed to provide immediate energy. Our bodies also release adrenaline, norepinephrine, and dopamine to keep our brains sharp and redirect blood flow to our brains for quick thinking. It is actually a brilliant mechanism. We have two to four minutes in any stressful situation where we or the perceived predator will win.

In a real life-or-death situation, the stress response will abate when the threat has passed. When the stress is ongoing, brought on by weighty and undigested issues, attachment to one's story, an inability to slow down, or negative self-talk, a low-level, prolonged stress response takes over our psyche.

A profound link exists between the central nervous system and metabolism—the rate at which your body assimilates and burns calories. The portion of the central nervous system that regulates gastric function is the autonomic nervous system. It is responsible for getting your stomach churning, getting the enzymes flowing, and keeping the nutrient absorption in the bloodstream going.

The autonomic nervous system also tells your body when to shut down digestion, such as when there is no food in your stomach or when you are in a fight-or-flight—that is, a stress—response.

The autonomic nervous system has two subdivisions that help it accomplish these tasks: the parasympathetic and the sympathetic nervous systems. Simply stated, when the parasympathetic nervous system is active, digestion is on, the stress response if off, and the body is relaxed. Let's call this "rest and digest." When the sympathetic nervous system is active, digestion turns off, stress response turns on, and the body is in fight-or-flight mode.

Our relationship with food often mirrors our relationship to life. Who are you when you sit down at the table? Are you a fast eater who sits down to a meal with multiple distractions? Are you associating mealtime with negative past experiences, stressful times, or a fear of gaining weight? Are you eating in response to feelings you want to numb yourself to, or are you eating in an effort to check out of a present situation?

Eating fast creates a stress response as that's not how our bodies are designed to receive food. Eating while distracted creates a stress response because our bodies don't have the opportunity to receive the sensory stimuli of the food to be digested.

If you are eating while running out of the house each morning or scarfing down a quick lunch, feeling pressure over where you have to be and not receiving pleasure from your food, the body hasn't a clue the stress it feels isn't life-threatening.

It is so very unfortunate that eating under stress has become commonplace and socially acceptable. The business of our lives often dictates eating on the run or lunching at our desks while managing several tasks at once.

Eating while under stress or with anxiety attached causes a multitude of digestive symptoms such as heartburn, cramping, and even prolonged hunger. Have you ever finished a meal under duress, unaware of having enjoyed it and felt as though it is just lying in your stomach? What you are feeling is accurate—it is.

The science of stress is multifaceted. The scientific documentation that connects weight gain, or the inability to lose weight is compelling. Many studies have shown that high cortisol production is strongly associated with fat accumulation. (1)

Chronic, low-level stress also increases the release of insulin, another hormone associated with weight gain. Insulin is responsible for removing glucose (blood sugar) from our bloodstream in an effort to create blood sugar balance. Insulin also tells the body to store excess carbohydrates as fat. Add this to the mix of the highly pleasurable, high-sugar, refined carbohydrates we reach for when stressed and anxious and we have a recipe for weight gain. As the situations that give rise to stress endure, they keep ramping up production of cortisol. It's as though you go into an inner Code Red, marked by anxiety. Depression can then ensue. At the same time, other survival tactics are activated by the psycho/physiological responses to the stress being experienced.

A newly discovered body-brain partnership sheds light on the behavior that often occurs when we are stressed, acutely and chronically: we seek chocolate, ice cream, and other sugar- and fat-laden treats not because they taste good but because the body is attempting to put a brake on the "runaway machinery of chronic stress."(2). The body has a lot of natural wisdom in its operations. It just wasn't designed to cope with long-term stress, nor with the enormity of Sub-Zero freezers or a bodega on every corner of every city.

The high fat- and sugar-laden treats become comfort foods in every sense of the word. Here is the paradox: these high-energy foods signal the brain to shut off the stress response and tell it that all is okay and you can relax. After the initial feel-good emotions wear off, we realize the consequences of our behavior. The shame and guilt set in, along with the digestive issues and uncomfortable fullness. We may even decide to purge in an effort to rid our bodies of what we thought was a solution. The cycle continues.

Being stressed about what food will do to us is counterproductive to our goals. The stress response we create over what we eat and what that food is going to do to our bodies brings consequences for mind, body, and spirit. Eating well is only half the story. How you eat—in other words, the state you are in when you eat—is the other half of the total picture for achieving a healthy and happy weight.

Here's another scenario. You are eating less and exercising more. You have been on numerous diets, and you can't seem to successfully lose those stubborn ten, twenty, or fifty pounds. You hate your body and believe you won't find happiness, love, or success until you lose that weight. You count every calorie and fat gram, reducing your intake to near starvation. You find no pleasure in going out for dinner because you have no trust in yourself not to devour an exorbitant amount of food. You feel deprived from all the restrictive rules you've put in place and can't stop staring at the bread basket. You are consumed with thoughts of food but fear what it will do to you.

The stress you feel here day after day is eating at you as it is all you think about. In this state, the salads and grilled chicken you are eating or the brownie or bowl of ice cream you are craving will have the same adverse effect on your weight-related goals. Eating while stressed or feeling guilty that you went off your diet robs us of any pleasure we deserve to receive from our food.

As digestion starts in our heads with the cephalic phase, distraction created by activity or even stressful thoughts doesn't allow our brains to recognize the sensory stimuli from our food. We miss the signals of the smells, tastes, and textures, and our brains don't signal our organs that food is coming. Not only do we miss any pleasure or satiety from it, we miss the fullness cues and can actually end up craving more.

If this feels familiar, no amount of restricting or punishing exercise will get you where you want to go. I see many clients who after years of dieting, restricting their calories, and avoiding specific food groups, still struggle with extra weight.

These are highly educated and sophisticated women and men who know what to eat in order to be healthy and maintain a happy and healthy weight. What comes up time after time is that they are surviving, although highly functioning, in a state of prolonged low-level stress. I am not talking about the stress that comes from the day-to-day routine of living, but the self-inflicted stress of what food will do *to* them.

I empathize; I am right there with them, because this is what I feared for much of my life. When we are engaged in the thought process that comes from limiting and toxic dietary beliefs, we trigger a stress response because our minds perceive food as the enemy. Remember, stress is the body's response to any threat, real or imagined. Several things happen in those four minutes it takes for the stress response to ignite: digestion slows, insulin and cortisol levels rise, our minds don't receive the message that the body is being nourished, and the result is nutrient excretion, poor digestion, slower metabolism, and the desire for more food.

When our food choices become a moral dilemma, stress results. When we eat questioning the nutritional value of our meal, stress results. When we admonish ourselves for what we ate, stress results. When we punish our bodies with exercise designed to make our bodies go away, stress results. When we look to a number on a scale to define us or set our mood for the day, stress results. If dinner is your largest meal of the day because you are tired and hungry from the day's events, you are going to store calories and fat, suffer poor digestion, and probably feel guilty and stressed over the meal. When we lose ourselves in the compulsive eating or the constant hunger we deny, stress results.

The bottom line is this: worrying about fat increases fat. Anxiety about weight loss causes your body to put fat on and retain it.

And then there is the low-level stress that comes from our everyday lives. Relationship issues, health issues, financial worries, caregiving, career- or school-related issues all play a role in how our bodies assimilate, digest, and metabolize. If you run out of the house in the morning grabbing a one-hundred-calorie, sugar-free, fat-free yogurt or a protein bar, you are negatively impacting your stress mechanism. If lunch is a five-minute experience at your desk or while driving to your next errand, your digestion and metabolism will suffer.

To simplify, the physical effects of a prolonged chronic low-level stress response are many:

- decreased blood flow to your stomach—as much as four times less
- 20,000-fold decrease in enzymatic output in your stomach, affecting how you assimilate the nutrients in your food
- increased digestive and gastric upset, such as heartburn, gas, bloating and cramping, constipation. and/or diarrhea
- decreased levels of growth hormone and thyroid hormone
- increased levels of insulin and cortisol
- decrease in amount of healthy gut bacteria
- excretion of minerals such as calcium and magnesium, contributing to bone loss
- excretion of the water-soluble vitamins B and C
- decreased oxygen intake
- increased inflammation, which is widely associated with disease
- decreased ability to burn calories

You can be eating the healthiest food on earth, but if you're eating while in a state of stress, you decrease the nutritional value of your food. We don't need to change the food; we need to change the eater.

The Relaxation Response and How It Frees Us

During the relaxation response, healing happens. In this state, our bodies can best experience the maintenance and repair of tissues.

Many people are surprised to learn that we can enjoy food without consequence. Our bodies function at optimal levels for digestion, assimilation of nutrients, metabolism and fat burning when relaxed. In this state of "rest and digest," the parasympathetic nervous system is in high gear, and we are more willing to accept uncertainty. We have trust and faith in the universe and its energy. We are connected to our higher self.

There has been a lot of talk about the "French paradox"—how the French can eat a diet consisting of meat, butter, full-fat cheese, desserts, and wonderful wine without suffering the consequences of obesity and related diseases. This was well documented in the best-seller, *French Women Don't Get Fat*. Early research pointed to compounds in the red wine as the force behind such good fortune, and thus vitamin manufacturers poured millions of dollars into isolating these compounds—polyphenols—and selling them over the counter in a supplement called resveratrol. The product was marketed as yet another answer to disease.

Looking at this scenario from another angle, the French eat while in a state of relaxation. They eat their largest meal midday and find enormous pleasure in a meal that consists of high-quality ingredients. They take several hours to eat it as they luxuriate in the company and surroundings that allow for true and total nourishment.

I witnessed this during our first visit to Paris. We arrived at our hotel before our room was ready. In an effort to pass time and acclimate, we went to the closest café. Sitting in the booth next to us was an older woman, elegantly dressed and beautifully coiffed. With perfect posture, she was totally immersed in her meal. I couldn't help but notice she was eating an omelet made from whole eggs, accompanied by buttered bread and a salad shimmering with an oil-based dressing. When she finished it all, the waiter removed her plate and replaced it with another that held a pastry. I was both in awe and shocked, as my immediate reaction was to question how she could be so slim. At this time, I was severely restricting my food intake, and it was beyond my wildest imagination that anyone could indulge this way and maintain such a trim body.

Have you experienced going on vacation where you eat and drink more than usual but return home having maintained or even lost weight? When removed from the stressors of our daily lives, we relax, and in so doing we achieve optimal calorie burning.

Letting go of tightly held stress allows us to create space and time. When we use that time to enjoy our meals, we can become relaxed eaters. As relaxed eaters, we receive true nourishment as we accept nurturing.

Bringing awareness to the table and practicing deep and conscious breathing is a useful tool. Breathing under stress is shallow and inconsistent. When we emerge from a stressful situation, we are likely to exhale deeply. That's because of the body's natural and innate instinct to automatically deeply breathe when it realizes a threat has passed. If we consciously start to take deep and rhythmic breaths while stressed, we fool our nervous system into believe we are actually in a relaxed state. Doing this sends a signal to the spinal nerves from the thinking center of the brain. The brain then deactivates the endocrine system, which is responsible for hormone production and release. The result is improved digestion, assimilation of nutrients, and maximum calorie burning.

Oxygen is fundamentally essential nutrient. The more we breathe, the more nourished we are. Take this to the table with you when you feel uncomfortable or are in a setting that doesn't lend itself to relaxed eating.

The solution lies in relaxing into your food as we relax into ourselves. How we eat and why we eat will have as much of an impact on our weight as what we eat; in some cases more of an impact.

Somewhere on the journey, so many of us have lost the notion that food, like life, is to be savored. Counting blessings instead of calories will contribute to creating a relaxation response. To deny our selves this is to deny our selves experiencing life in its entirety.

Since there is no life without stress, resilience must be acquired, if not learned in order to achieve a state of relaxation. Resilience is the ability to adapt well in the face of adversity, trauma, or stress. While psychological resilience has been well studied in the field of disasters, it is also applicable to recovering from disordered eating behaviors, which requires many life-changing shifts. Just as with a devastating hurricane or traumatic life-cycle event, the behaviors that accompany compulsive eating can affect our physical, emotional, cognitive, biological, and spiritual well-being, as well as our friends and family.

Much research points to the idea that we have inherent abilities to be resilient, but we can incorporate certain behaviors, thoughts, and actions in building skills of resilience. These include accepting the adversity, choosing to have hope, changing our thinking, making connections, embracing actions, and learning from the adversity. (3)

Often we resist relaxing and slowing down at meals. Doing so can be uncomfortable if it brings up upsetting feelings we can't control. When we have spent a lifetime in a routine, changing it will be uncomfortable. We will feel a strong pull back to the familiar, even if it brings us pain.

My addictive behaviors were overwhelming and often felt insurmountable. I was traumatized, barely functioning even though outwardly I was going through the motions of my life. The effect on me physically and on my relationships with family in particular made it an extremely difficult road to travel. Once I was able to step outside myself and step back from my focus on food and body, I could embrace the hope that I could rewrite my story. I gave myself permission to look at my beliefs about food and my body as the myths and lies they were. As I sit here writing about that time, I find myself taking deep breaths, remembering the tension I had within me. I can feel the stress leave my body now as it was so necessary to let go of then.

Letting go of the fear-induced stress ended the vicious cycle. Fear of what the food would do to me led to stress and anxiety, creating a response that triggered me to seek comfort. Today instead of thinking comfort food, I think peaceful food—what can I eat that will make me feel at peace, beloved, and nurtured in the healthy sense? To eat differently than that just doesn't make any sense to me anymore. It is extremely empowering to realize that I can face stress and adversity in a healthy way rather than becoming powerless to it. There is no life without pain, no light without darkness. Finding ways to cope that will nurture you is essential to healing.

Slowing down with food is metaphoric to slowing down our lives. We can relax into our bodies as we relax into our relationships, our work lives, and the uncertainty that may surround us when life happens.

Relaxing into life allows us to experience freedom as we take back our time and our integrity to self and find a safe and sacred space within ourselves to call home.

Embrace It

- **Practice Breathing.** This is a simple technique that works well. Exhale deeply, feeling all the air go out of your lungs. Feel the breath to your core. Place the tip of your tongue at the front of your palate, just behind your front teeth, and inhale through your nose for a count of four. Hold it for a count of seven and deeply exhale for a count of eight. Repeat this process four times, and do it throughout the day.
- **Dine with people who nourish and comfort you,** engaging in conversation that is free of negativity.
- **Use positive thoughts and affirmations** as you prepare and enjoy your meal.
- **Seek out relaxation techniques** that stimulate the same pleasure centers in the brain that makes us seek "comfort" food. Experiment with various techniques to see what works for you. Examples are pleasurable exercise, dance, meditation, yoga, hot baths, and, of course, sex.

Journal It

How do you show up in your relationship with food?
Do you manage stress with food, or do you manage food stressfully?

_____

_____

_____

_____

_____

_____

_____

_____

_____

_____

_____

_____

_____

_____

Affirm It

Being calm and centered is one of my top priorities, and I practice feeling it every day.

Being calm and relaxed energizes my whole being as it washes over me with every breath I take.

All negativity is evaporating from my body and my mind.

All my muscles are becoming more and more relaxed as they release the tensions I have been holding on to. As I relax, my body immediately feels better.

A relaxed mind and body are more apt to be a present mind and body.

Read More about It

Marc David, *The Slow Down Diet: Eating for Pleasure, Energy and Weight Loss*, Healing Arts Press, 2005

Mark Hyman, *The Ultra Mind Solution*, USA, Simon and Schuster, 2009

CHAPTER 3

Eat When You're Hungry, Stop When You've Had Enough

Hunger brought mood swings and food swings. When hungry I had to deal with food choices and the constant reminders of how fearful I was that food would make me fat. It always reminded me how even the simplest decision to eat made me uncomfortable. On the flip side were the euphoric feelings that came with hunger, for it meant I was still in control and hadn't overeaten. Such madness.

I have experienced denying my hunger as a restrictive eater, and I have fed emotional hungers with compulsive eating and overeating. When I was restricting, I spent hours counting calories and grams of fat and carbohydrates. I was terrified of what food would do to me. I had my own set of rules and conditions for what I would allow myself to eat. I used my relationship with food to control and manage my insecurities and fear of feeling. When I was engaging in compulsive eating behaviors, I ate mindlessly, looking through the pantry for "something" to fill me up, help me check out, or take the edge off my anxiety.

Family birthday celebrations were a great example of this kind of back-and-forth behavior. The Carvel ice cream cakes were our go-to birthday dessert. I had such a love/hate relationship with those cakes. Convinced I would become my own version of "Fudgie the Whale" if I indulged, I would serve the cake to our guests and take my piece last. I always had a slice lest I be "the mom" who wouldn't enjoy a piece of cake on her daughter's or husband's birthday. I could have been eating razor blades as I envisioned each mouthful ending up on my thighs. Stressed out over what the cake would do to me, I couldn't enjoy the deliciousness of it or even focus on the joyful occasion we were celebrating.

The irony is that after the party was over and I was alone in the kitchen cleaning up, I would find myself standing, knife in hand, at the cake, slicing slivers of icing and chocolate cookie crunchies into my mouth. I was totally checked out, craving more of what I had mindlessly eaten, ignoring any messages of hunger or fullness.

Understanding true physical hunger, toxic hunger, and emotional hunger is part of the foundation for developing a healthy relationship with food.

Physical Hunger

Let's look at what happens to make us hungry. Our bodies, when left to their devices, are brilliantly efficient. Hunger regulation is a function of fuel in and energy out. A system of brain chemicals signal the body when to eat, and when we have enough stored energy, we get the signal to stop. An appetite stimulant called ghrelin is released when a part of the brain called the hypothalmus senses that the body is low on energy, i.e. fuel. Along with ghrelin, the hormone insulin regulates hunger levels, and leptin produces feelings of fullness and satiety to make us stop eating.

For many chronic dieters, hunger becomes just another feeling to ignore. We become so efficient at suppressing hunger that we numb our innate ability to trust or respect this inherent signal as a natural biological process. We have forgotten that food can be a source of pleasure as well as nourishment. We forget that food is foremost a primary source of nourishment long before we determine it to be pleasure, punishment, or even a source of pain.

As newborns, the first experiences of love and nurturing occur as we are cuddled and fed. Later on, we develop the wonderful associations with food through memories of a beloved grandmother or holiday tradition. These associations can easily translate to unhealthy habits in the way we relate to stress so that they becomes distorted. At some time, we may come home from a bad day and devour bags of cookies or chips. The mind records the process as: feel bad > eat > feel better. The hunger signal is lost, and the next time we have a bad day, our minds remember this useful behavior. We have learned to seek temporary pleasure in order to avoid immediate pain. This temporary pleasure we receive is chemical, as the food choices we make when stressed have a direct effect on our mood. The highly refined, high-sugar foods create a blood sugar response that is powerful because it creates the sensations of pleasure and relaxation. When the blood sugar response subsides, painful emotions return, we go back for more soothing, and a destructive cycle ensues.

When I refused to give in to my body's hunger, essentially going hungry all day, ignoring any demand for food and nourishment, I set myself up for episodes of binge eating. I would play a numbers game with myself—how few calories could I eat before dinner? Breakfast was a measured bowl of cereal and skim milk, maybe a few strawberries. At midmorning I would have some more coffee to keep going, and lunch would be a small salad with a fat-free dressing or maybe a fat-free yogurt. If I made it through the afternoon without grabbing something from the pantry, finishing my children's after-school snack, or even munching on that night's dinner preparations, I would be getting the screaming message of how hungry I was when finally relaxing at the end of the day. Dinner became the largest meal of the day, and I usually overate until I was stuffed and uncomfortable. After dinner I would indulge on the salty, sweet, creamy, or crunchy foods that brought relief from the stress of the day. I would fall asleep uncomfortably full and vow to be better tomorrow.

There is no benefit in not listening to our bodies. We must learn to include them in the conversation because our minds will keep us tied to the toxic beliefs that food will make us fat or that fat and carbs will make us fat. Eventually, however, our bodies will speak up and let us know they needs those nutrients to keep our brains functioning and hormones flowing. Eating when hungry, tuning in to our bodies' signals for nourishment, improves the chances that we won't end up holding an empty container of ice cream after a day of trying to be "good."

When we diet in a way that restricts the food that gives us pleasure, or act on the thoughts and beliefs that actually create nutritional deprivation, we are going to crave the foods our bodies truly need for energy, and we are going to crave the foods we've deemed "illegal," such as fats and carbohydrates. By not trusting our hunger, we set ourselves up to feel deprived, like failures at dieting, and ultimately powerless over food. Identify the craving and listen to it. Hunger tells us it is time to eat, and cravings will tell us what to eat.

Eating when hungry and stopping when we have had enough is more about the *how* of eating than the *what*. The *what* changes constantly as the field of nutrition science continues to discover and assign new "rules." The *how* should be constant, whether we are eating chicken or enchiladas. It is empowering to choose our food wisely, eat in a slow rhythm so we can enjoy it and get satisfaction, and relax into it so we can digest and assimilate the nutrients and become energized as our bodies reap the benefits.

Emotional Hunger

We eat emotionally to look for comfort in emotionally charged situations. Our desire is actually not for the food but for the emotion it creates. It is important to differentiate and then put space between our behavior and the feelings. For example, we often look to food to distract us from boredom and emotional turmoil.

When my late husband, Stuart, was being treated in the hospital for cancer, I spent many hours alone because he was asleep or semiconscious from the medicines. I would walk the halls and invariably end up in the cafeteria. Filling up on bitter coffee, salads that were totally unsatisfying, apples that were mealy, stale bagels, and sugar-laden yogurts was a way to pass the time. I wasn't hungry. I was bored, fearful, grieving, and lonely. Healthier solutions would have been for me to call a friend, write in my journal, or visit the chapel in an effort to face what I was really feeling.

We sometimes look to food when we really need a hug, a human connection, and to experience security and intimacy. These "cravings" come from another part of our selves that could be starving for love, connection, and fulfillment.

We often turn to food as we celebrate a joyous event, such as celebrating a job promotion with chocolate and champagne. Food is always part of life-cycle event celebrations, and often we overindulge because we aren't accustomed to allowing ourselves to receive pleasure from food on a daily basis.

Several differences exist between emotional hunger and physical hunger. I point this out because often we don't know the difference, especially if we have been denying our true hungers for a long time.

Emotional hunger appears suddenly and needs to be satisfied instantly, while physical hunger happens gradually and you can wait to eat.

When you eat to fill an emptiness that is not your stomach calling out, you crave a specific food, such as pizza or ice cream. When you eat because you are actually hungry, you are open to options.

When eating in response to emotion or stress, you are likely to eat beyond being full. When eating to satisfy a healthy hunger, you are more likely to stop when you recognize you are satisfied and full.

Toxic Hunger

Toxic hunger refers to the withdrawal symptoms that occur from eating foods with little nutritional value. These symptoms occur when we are experiencing the lower end of the blood-sugar curve, and they drive our bodies to eat more than we need in response to cravings, leading to weight gain and certainly making weight loss more difficult.

If you are reading this book, chances are you have been eating a diet rich in foods that are "light," fat-free, sugar-free, and essentially fake. Typical symptoms of toxic hunger are:

- feelings of emptiness in the stomach
- gurgling and rumbling in the stomach
- dizziness, lightheadedness, and headache
- irritability and agitation
- lack of concentration
- nausea, shakiness, and fatigue

True hunger, as opposed to toxic hunger, signals when our bodies need calories to maintain energy levels and lean body mass. When we eat in response to our body's wisdom, we won't become overweight to begin with.

In our present toxic food environment, many of us have lost the ability to connect with that wisdom and the signals that tell us how much to eat and what kind of food we really need. The way back from a relationship with food that is mired in toxicity and confusion lies in examining our beliefs and food patterns, questioning if they are serving us, and making an empowered choice to change.

Cravings

Sometimes hunger shows up in the form of cravings—and cravings show up in response to extreme hunger.

Cravings are our bodies' way of signaling that something is missing—such as an underlying health concern that needs to be addressed or a biochemical and nutritional piece you may be lacking. Often we crave sugar when we really need protein or sleep. Salt cravings may be signs that you need rare minerals like potassium, chromium, or copper. You may need to incorporate more mineral-rich foods into your diet like nuts, seeds, and sea vegetables. Chocolate cravings may indicate you need more iron or magnesium; you may need to eat more leafy greens like kale or bok choy.

Your cravings may also be a bigger-than-life question that needs a new answer. Are you hearing, "I need chocolate," when you could be seeking spirituality, sensuality, movement, fun, or creativity? That piece of cake may mean you desire more sweetness in your life. Truthfully, it is easier to reach for the bag of M&Ms than to dig deep and bypass the feeling of comfort that comes from being in the zone of familiarity. "Cravings" that are triggered by emotional responses are not about food. When we experience a craving, it helps to get curious and ask what is out of balance.

Use the following checklist the next time you have a craving in order to figure out what you are truly "hungry" for:

- When was the last time you ate?
- Did your meal or snack have enough protein, fat, or carbohydrates?
- Did you sleep well last night?
- Is there anything physiological going on such as PMS?
- Are you drinking enough water?
- Did something happen in your day to frustrate you?
- Do you need to discuss something with your spouse/ partner?

Cravings, like hunger, are not signs of weakness. They are valuable and vital messages meant to help you find balance. Basically, we need to trust our bodies instead of ignoring and denying what are natural, biological, and psychological processes of being.

What Is a Normal Eater?

People ask me this all the time. I believe no such person exists. We can be healthy eaters, those who have a healthy relationship with food as opposed to people who only eat healthy food.

Some eat three meals a day, and others eat 4—6 smaller meals. Some can skip a meal when busy or be that picky restaurant diner who needs to make sure her menu selection is prepared as she wishes.

Some are extremely conscious of nutrition while others just eat what is available. Some may overeat on special occasions and others rarely overeat because food just doesn't matter that much to them. Some prepare elaborate meals for family and friends, and others have the local takeout places on speed dial. What all healthy eaters have in common is the following:

- They eat when they are hungry or have a craving.
- They choose foods that will satisfy them.
- They eat with awareness and stay connected to their bodies.
- They stop eating when they are full or satisfied.

Earlier, I said that *how* we eat is as important as *what* we eat. Having a healthy relationship with food means we are not defined *by how* much, *how* little, *or how* often we eat. Healthy eaters recognize and respond appropriately to their hunger. Respecting their hunger, listening to what it's asking for, and including their bodies in the conversation allows them to choose satisfying food. Healthy eaters don't choose based on the calculation of fat and calories. They don't wait until they are starving or eat if they aren't hungry. They make their own menu selections, rather than getting what the person across the table orders.

The good news is that we can relearn to tune in to our body's wisdom and develop a healthier relationship with food as we begin to trust our hungers and in turn trust our bodies.

When we are satisfied, we can stop when we've had enough. Feeling full and feeling satisfied are separate but related reactions to hunger and the experience of eating. When we lose touch with our body's needs, it is hard to know when it has had enough of anything, especially food.

Sometimes the distortion stems from a message we received in childhood that we needed to finish everything on our plates because there were children starving in China, or because our mothers slaved for hours over a hot stove. Maybe your parents grew up during the Great Depression, so they taught you to clean your plate quickly since food could easily be scarce. In cases like these, we as children weren't allowed to respond and react to our bodies' signals for fullness and satiety. We grew into adults who are unable to recognize such signals or willfully ignore them. We learned to base our sense of enough on external cues—portion size, whatever we can get away with, what we feel we deserve, media messages, or even the approval of those with whom we are eating.

Maybe you felt you needed to be a certain weight or size in order to be accepted into the sorority of your dreams; maybe the messages you received growing up were that no one would love you if you weren't thin enough; maybe your spouse or partner has indicated that he or she is not attracted to people who are overweight; maybe your extra weight is offering you protection from being seen and heard; maybe you have dieted yourself down to a certain weight so you can feel either invisible or powerful. In an effort to seek safety, love, and belonging, we often manipulate our food intake so we can get what we want.

By not honoring our hungers in an authentic way, we lose sight of the bigger picture—that we are actually seeking nourishment that reflects how we want to experience life.

The first step toward developing a healthy relationship with food is to give our selves permission to eat anything. This may sound counterproductive, but when we take the moral dilemma away from our meal planning and snack choices, we rid ourselves of the shame and guilt that results from depending on willpower alone.

The next step is to rely on hunger and fullness cues. The third step is to eat for physical rather than emotional or stress-related reasons. Making decisions about when and what to eat based on what our body is experiencing creates a sense of empowerment. Empowerment comes from asking ourselves if the food we are choosing to eat will truly satisfy and sustain us. It is empowering to be accountable to the experience we want from the meal.

For example, if you were hungry for lunch and chose to drink a smoothie, will it hold you until your next meal? Would just a salad do the trick, or would you enjoy some chicken with that? This practice should also be extended to food that is ordinarily on our "should not eat" list. If you have a sweet tooth, will an apple satisfy?

It's been said that how we do one thing is how we do everything, and this is true of how we eat. Your relationship with food will mirror how you work, relate to people, and take care of yourself. Not knowing when we have had enough to eat can mean we don't know how to effectively use the words *yes* and *no*. A restrictive eater says no too often; a compulsive, emotional eater says yes too often. The goal is to strike a healthy balance. We can experience great discomfort in learning to say no and yes to ourselves and to others. But developing that muscle will introduce you to the concept of integrity to self, inspiring and motivating you to move closer to the loving, joyful, and healthy life you deserve and desire.

Embrace It

- When you want to eat and you are not hungry, ask yourself, **"What is it I really want?"** Acknowledge that you may want to be with someone and you are alone, or maybe you are with someone and want to be alone. Practice being present, experience what is happening within you; when you can be out of your head, separate from your thoughts. If it can be satisfied with something other than food, it is not hunger.

- **Remember that hunger is a survival mechanism.** Even if you have checked out from allowing yourself to feel physical hunger, know that it is there. Before you eat, rate your hunger by creating an intuitive inner scale from one to five. One is noticing hunger and five is starving. Plan to eat when you are at a two or three. Food tastes best when you are moderately hungry.

- **Recognize when you have had enough.** Also create a fullness scale from one to five. Stop when you are at a three or four, nourished and energized, satisfied but not stuffed. At that point, push your plate away or, if you can, leave the table (you don't want to abandon your dinner companions). If you are eating out, ask the server to remove your plate.

Journal It

What would it be like for you if you ate only when you were physically hungry?

_____

_____

_____

_____

_____

_____

_____

_____

_____

_____

_____

_____

_____

Affirm It

I happily nourish my body and receive full satisfaction for moderate meals daily.

I listen to my body and eat only when I am hungry, staying in control of what and when I eat.

I am starting to realize food is not the answer to my problems.

I need not rely on willpower, as I am becoming empowered to transform into someone who is responsible with food.

I successfully release the need for food that makes me uncomfortable as I release the desire to eat beyond the point of being full.

Read More about It

Geneen Roth, *When Food Is Love*, New York, Plume, The Penguin Group, 1992

Evelyn Tribole and Elyse Resch, *Intuitive Eating*, New York, St. Martin's Griffin, 1995

Karen Koenig, *Rules of Normal Eaters: A Commonsense Approach for Dieters, Overeaters, Undereaters, Emotional Eaters, and Everyone In Between*, California, Gurze Books, 2005

Marc David, *Nourishing Wisdom*, New York, Bell Tower, harmony Books, 1991

CHAPTER 4

Eat Mindfully, Without Distraction

For me it was madness as opposed to mindfulness. I vividly remember preparing dinner for my family during my severe restricting days. On the night that burns so brightly in my memory, I was preparing a pasta dinner. While setting out all of the ingredients, I read on the side of the box that a serving size weighed two ounces. Out came the food scale, and I discovered that thirty pieces of penne weighed two ounces. I decided I would allow myself to eat fifteen. While my family and I were seemingly enjoying dinner together, I was lost in my head, counting each piece of pasta that went into my mouth. What resulted was another lost conversation, another lost opportunity to connect with the loves of my life, and another example of compulsion taking over; what we try to control, controls us.

Friends and clients often tell me how much they have to do, and I often feel the same stress. We have errands, emails to read and respond to, the responsibilities to the business of our lives, work, and the demands of our relationships. These to-do lists create the feeling that there just isn't enough time in the day. We end up eating as we run out the door, in the car, in front of the TV or computer, while on the phone, standing in front of the refrigerator, standing at the stove, or while clearing the table. The result is there is no chance of pleasure or calm. We need to clear the clutter.

When we eat mindfully, without distraction, we can appreciate and derive pleasure from our food. Eating becomes an experience where we can engage our senses. Pleasure is a huge part of the equation when finding freedom with food. When there is pleasure there is no guilt, no shame, and no fear.

Eating mindfully, without distraction, allows us to discover and savor the sight, smell, texture, and taste of our food. By slowing down, we can fully experience the elements of our food, creating awareness of and satiety with appropriate portions.

Eating mindfully, soulfully, allows us to develop a healthy, and ultimately a wonderful, relationship with food.

Many of us restrict in an effort to control our weight. Sometimes we abuse food, using it to distract us from uncomfortable feelings. When we use food in either of these ways, we ignore the *pleasure* food can bring us, as we swallow it before we even taste it.

What would your life be like if you treated food and your body as you would a loved one—with patience, gentleness, playfulness, communication, honesty, respect, and love?

The Science of Mindfulness

The concept of mindfulness can be traced back to the ancient Buddhist philosophy of meditation. The goal of this concept is to create a heightened awareness of one's behaviors, thoughts, and emotions without any judgment.

Mindful eating is not about being obsessed with food choices or counting calories. Mindfulness is becoming aware of mind and body signals every time you eat. When you eat mindfully, you can observe different body cues that influence how, what, and when you eat.

Eating mindfully, with awareness, is powerful. It slows you down so you can honor your hunger and satiety. It creates the relaxation response that enhances digestion, nutrient assimilation, and calorie burning.

These functions actually begin in the mind. Scientists call it the cephalic phase digestive response—CPDR. *Cephalic* means "of the head." This phase of digestion is simply a more sophisticated way of identifying the pleasures of taste, smell, satiety, and the visual component of a meal. It actually is about how our minds digest what we are eating. Researchers estimate that 30–40% of the total digestive response to any meal is due to CPDR, the mental awareness of what we are eating.

Digestion begins in the mind as chemical and mechanical receptors on the tongue and in the mouth and nose are stimulated by smelling, tasting, chewing, and simply noticing food. A true awareness of our meal begins the secretion of saliva, stomach acid, and enzymes and stimulates neuropeptides and production of the full range of pancreatic enzymes. At the same time, blood rushes to the digestive organs, the stomach and intestines begin to rhythmically contract, and electrolyte concentrations get ready to receive the incoming food.

When we are not aware of our meal and the eating experience, neglecting to register any of the tastes, smells, satiety, or visual cues, we are only digesting and metabolizing at 60–70 percent of our capacity. This translates into less efficient digestion, nutrient absorption, and metabolism.

A research study recently involved something called "dichotomous listening." Here, researchers asked test subjects to listen as two people talked simultaneously—one person talked into the subject's left ear about space travel while the other talked in his or her right ear about the joys of financial freedom.

When the test subjects were in a relaxed state and not listening to the speakers, the researchers gave them a mineral drink. They measured the absorption of two minerals, sodium and chloride, in the subjects' small intestines and discovered they experienced 100% assimilation. When the test subjects were exposed to dichotomous listening and given their mineral drink, they didn't absorb any of the minerals. The simple act of experiencing two stimuli at once had a dramatic effect on their metabolisms. (1)

When our attention is directed outside of our bodies, we can't possibly experience the physical sensations connected with food. We can't sense when we are full, the deliciousness of the food, or even if we don't like it.

When we question what we are eating, focusing our awareness on the fat and calories we perceive to be in our food, we can't be mindful of the food or the experience. As when we talk to a friend who isn't paying attention, we leave the experience feeling incomplete and wanting more.

The cephalic phase digestive response is actually a nutritional requirement. The brain must experience taste, pleasure, aroma, and satisfaction in order to assess and begin our most efficient digestive force. When we eat too fast or neglect to notice our food, the brain interprets this missed experience as hunger. We then reach for more food. The less awareness we bring to the table, the more we will need to eat. When we eat while distracted by outside stimuli, we don't even taste the food. Our brain screams, "I want more."

The same phenomenon occurs when we are distracted with thoughts of guilt, shame, and fear over our food choices. Our bodies will not notice the donut, piece of chocolate, or bowl of pasta. What we thought we wanted can't bring any satisfaction; it's hard to empower ourselves with choice when we don't really let ourselves have it in the first place.

One of the most effective strategies for developing a healthy relationship with food through mindfulness is embodiment. Embodiment allows us to inhabit our bodies so we can honor and respect the space where we can feel relaxed and empowered. In this space we experience pleasure. In this space we feel present to the heightened physical sensations of eating without guilt or shame about what we are eating.

Practicing mindfulness and embodiment at the table keeps us from using food to check out. Embodiment reflects the wisdom of our bodies and how aligned we are with them. We can only eat what we want, when we want it when we include our bodies in the conversation. To rely on anything external such as the scale or a distorted image of our selves distracts from mindfulness and embodiment.

Like the eater who has a healthy relationship with food and hunger, the mindful eater automatically checks in with his or her body for fullness and satiety cues. Even when these eaters are multitasking, they are aligned with their bodies' messages because the signals are clear and can be trusted. Mindful, healthy eaters breathe during the meal, chew well before swallowing, and pause often to enjoy the taste of the food. They focus on the food in front of them rather than what they may have eaten earlier in the day or have planned to eat tomorrow.

Mindful eating introduces us to a new level of freedom. Relying on the natural intelligence of our bodies empowers us to trust ourselves and embrace the deliciousness of what food and eating can do for us. Mindful eating actually opens us up to the possibility of developing not only a healthy relationship with food but a loving one.

Let me be clear. As compulsive eaters, we are not lovers of food. Craving, obsessing over, binging, and restricting are not behaviors that reflect love. Eating this way, motivated by fear, guilt, or a need to check out from the day is indicative of a loss of control brought about by negative self-talk and shame. We don't let ourselves enjoy food because we not only fear what it will do to us, but we don't think we are allowed to enjoy it. So we eat the grilled chicken breast or burger without the bun and then find many other ways to eat what we really want while we distract ourselves from the reality that we are eating.

Whatever we weigh, we are entitled to find pleasure and joy in our food, just as we are entitled to find pleasure and joy in all we do.

Loving food is to smell it, taste it, and savor it. A love affair with food gives new meaning to eating emotionally. That's right, you are reading correctly—emotional eating can be wonderful. Eating with emotion as opposed to eating in order to deal with emotion is incredible. When you eat, eat and experience the wonder and complexity of food as you experience freedom.

Several months ago, I came across a recipe for a vegetarian chili—for me a *pleasure* food. I stashed the recipe on the kitchen counter and finally set out to prepare it for dinner on a wintry night last week. After shopping for and preparing the ingredients, I tasted, seasoned, tasted again, simmered and stirred, and tasted again. I was delighted with the result.

What's the Big Deal, You Ask?

It wasn't too long ago, after spending the better part of my adult life restricting, eating compulsively, and consistently purging, that I was able to recognize that the obsession with food, dieting, and my body had lifted. This glorious pot of soul-warming, simmering chili represented that for me. Gone were the calculating thoughts regarding calories, fat, protein, and carbs. Instead, I was focused on the taste, texture, and downright deliciousness of what was going to be my meal. As my senses were heightened, so was my sense of self. With this came the realization that I no longer needed to be the smallest person in the room or judge myself by the size of my thighs. I developed a sense of self that propelled me to want to be bigger, in spirit, to actually take up more space on this blessed earth. I no longer feared what the food would do to me and fully embraced what food could do for me.

The next time you reach for "comfort food," think about what will bring peace and pleasure to your soul, eat it with awareness and without guilt, and enjoy all the healing and nourishment it brings you.

Who Woulda Thunk It Chili

Prep time: 10 minutes
Prep notes: You can buy your onion peppers and butternut squash precut
Cooking time: 45 minutes
Yields: 6 people

Ingredients:

- 1 cup onion, chopped
- 4 cloves garlic, chopped or minced
- 2 bell peppers (1 green and 1 red)
- 1/2–1 jalapeño, seeded and diced
- 4 cups of butternut squash, cubed
- 4 15 oz. cans of beans, rinsed and drained (I used two cans of red kidney, one each of black and pinto)
- 1/2 bunch cilantro, chopped
- 2 tablespoons chili powder
- 1 tablespoon cumin
- 1 15 oz. can Muir Glen fire roasted diced tomatoes
- 4 cups vegetable broth
- 1/2 bunch kale, stems removed and leaves chopped
- 1 tablespoon olive oil
- Sea salt and pepper to taste

Directions:

- Heat olive oil in a large pot over medium heat. Stir in onion, garlic, and jalapeno along with a pinch of salt. Allow to cook for 3–5 minutes.
- Stir in peppers and cook for another 3 minutes. Add squash, chili powder, and cumin. Give it a good stir.
- Add beans, tomatoes, and broth. Turn heat to high and bring soup to a boil. Once boiling, reduce to a simmer and cook until the squash is tender—about 20 minutes. Check the consistency of the soup. For a thicker soup, continue to simmer for another 15 minutes or so.

Add kale to the pot and cover for about 5 minutes or until it wilts down. Give everything one last stir, taste, and adjust seasoning. Add the cilantro and enjoy!

Serve this with side bowls of guacamole and toasted corn tortillas, Greek yogurt, sour cream, and shredded cheese, if desired.

Adapted from *Clean and Delicious.* By Dani Spies

Embrace It

- **Eat while sitting at the table, without distractions.** This means eating without the distractions from TV, newspaper, computer, triggering conversations, or loud music. When your attention is on something other than the food on your plate, it won't be on what's going on in your body.

- If you are a fast eater, **slow down.** If you normally eat breakfast in five minutes, stretch it to ten. If you eat lunch in ten minutes, stretch it to fifteen. It may be helpful to set a timer.

- **Let go of any negative thoughts and judgments** you may have about the food you want to eat. Instead, focus on the positive values—for example healthy fat will make my skin soft and my hair shiny.

- **Become aware** of the smell, taste, and texture of the food as you focus on the positive energy you will gain form the experience of eating.

- View it as though it has no name. Can you see the energy that emanates from the food?

- **Bring the food up to your nose,** smell it, and describe the experience.

- Before you put the food in your mouth, **notice** how your tongue produces saliva. Notice the mind/body reaction and how your senses respond to the anticipation you eating the food.

- Experience **touching** your food.

- **Notice** how your hand knows just how to get the food into your mouth. Notice how your tongue reacts and knows how to receive the food every time.

- As you **slowly** bite into the food, **start to chew.** Notice how your tongue decides which side you will chew on. Give all your attention to your mouth. Then stop and experience the explosion of taste. Notice and describe if it is sweet or bitter, salty, or sour.

- **Swallow your food completely** before you take another bite.

- **Be aware** of the consistency. **Notice** how it changes.
- Be sure to **breathe**, pausing for a minute or two. Bring the same quality of attention to the breath that you gave to seeing, feeling, smelling, and tasting the food.
- **Observe** everything about the meal that **nourishes**—the people you are with, your surroundings, and the conversation you're having or listening to. Be present and become aware of how present you are. Let go of judgmental thoughts about the food you are about to eat.

Journal It

Eating without any distraction would mean _____

_____

_____

_____

_____

_____

_____

_____

_____

_____

_____

_____

_____

_____

_____

_____

_____

Affirm It

As I enjoy the color, smells, and taste of the food I happily choose to eat, I enjoy the color, smells, and feel of life around me.

I am aware of how my thoughts can affect my behavior with food. I will reject the social messages I receive about weight and food, trusting I know what is best for my body.

Every day I get better at making healthy food choices I am comfortable with, and I eat slowly and mindfully, paying close attention to each bite so I can stop when I am satisfied.

When I notice an absence of mind, I slowly and gently return to the experience of here and now. I am willing and loving in doing so.

I can meet my thoughts, feelings, and impulses without getting lost in them.

Read More about It

Marc David, *The Slow Down Diet: Eating for Pleasure, Energy and Weight Loss,* Vermont, Healing Arts Press, 2005

CHAPTER 5

Do Something Everyday That Makes Your Body Feel Alive

First there was Michael, then Ralph, Kenny, and Frankie. Later there was Matt, Jose, Robert, and some whose names I forget. They all served a purpose—to get me to the point where I could feel good in and about my body, but I was going about it all wrong. I wanted to please, be a star, and was shameless in my flirting.

These men were my personal trainers through various times in my thirties and forties.

Michael was my first. He was so good-looking. He was chiseled with the tightest tush I had ever seen on a man. Small in stature, his presence was huge, and he had the following to prove it. He taught aerobic and weight-lifting classes at a local exercise studio. I decided I was going to get healthier, and improve my shrinking body, by enrolling in them.

Michael's classes were really fun. He played music that made you want to move, and he was extremely charismatic. Very quickly, I found myself wanting to be one of his groupies; after all, I could be as svelte and toned as any of the women in the class. Or could I? Insecurity followed me like a sad puppy. I was constantly comparing and judging myself. Was I agile enough? Could I handle enough weight? Was I hot, thin, or beautiful enough to earn a place in the front row of Michael's class?

A short while after I began that routine, it was abruptly interrupted. I was shopping for outdoor garbage cans, and a freak accident caused a stack of 4–32 lb. cans to fall from an overhead shelf and land on my left shoulder. I was badly bruised, suffered internal injuries, and was later diagnosed with a torn rotator cuff. The orthopedist I saw in the days after the accident told me how lucky I was to have such a strong muscle girdle surrounding my shoulder. If I hadn't been working out, my shoulder could have been shattered. This was the first time I was able to connect wellness with exercise. For me, exercise had been a means to make my body go away. At that point, I saw there was more to it and that it could be a means for me to be stronger and healthier, more powerful. I now had professional validation to continue my quest for a stronger body; however, I still desired that body to be leaner.

Unable to continue with the workout routine I had fallen into, I began physical therapy and pushed myself to my limits and beyond. I finally required surgery to repair my rotator cuff and eventually resumed my compulsive exercising. I hung on to the insight I had gained, but soon I was back to using the guise of fitness as a way to have the "perfect" body. Exercising was still about the size of my thighs.

I went from gym to gym, trainer to trainer. The harder they pushed, the more accomplished I felt. One of the trainers kept red garbage pails nearby, as he was known for taking his trainees to the point of needing to vomit. My relationship with him ended as I realized the stress of working out with him was taking a toll on my body and my emotions.

Part of my recovery process was letting go of the need for and idea of "perfectionism." Learning to accept things as they are and being present allowed me to ease up on the rigorous routine I was *in. It was so freeing with respect to energy and time I gained in my day. For a while, I stayed out of the gym. I started walking outdoors and would often meet a friend for an hour-long walk. I could finally feel that I was exercising for the love of movement, being outdoors, and feeling connected to a beloved friend. I realized I don't like the treadmill, or other apparatuses designed to have me move in ways that just don't feel good to my body.*

I discovered Pilates and yoga and learned that these methods are best for me because they promote embodiment and a connection to the part of me that is most at peace. I discovered a Pilates studio near my office, so it is very convenient to go there to exercise when I have a break or before or after office hours. My instructors gently take me through the moves in a way that gets me to focus on posture and strength. I also go to a neighborhood gym once a week to work out with Debora, a fabulous woman who is really smart, well-educated on the workings of the body, and respects my needs as a maturing woman. We have fun and talk about our kids, recipes, and books we are reading for the book club we attend together.

I move in a way that honors my body and engage in movement to keep my bones healthy and my mind clear. It's not about disappearing or being the teacher's pet. It's about embracing this blessed life I have and being an active participant in it.

True freedom from an unhealthy relationship with food cannot happen without our ability and willingness to connect to and inhabit our bodies. When we let our bodies speak and we listen, we are naturally drawn to behaviors, and foods, that help us to thrive, be nourished, and feel nourished. This connection is what is known as *embodiment*.

Movement is a wonderful way to inhabit the body and connect to its wisdom. Movement is natural; our bodies want to do it and must do it in order to thrive. If you listen to your body, you will find that it craves movement. We will also quickly degenerate without it. The adage, "If you don't use it, you'll lose it," is absolutely true, as our muscles will atrophy—diminish in size and strength—when not put to use.

I experienced this recently when my lower leg was in a cast after foot surgery. When the cast was removed after just two weeks of not using my leg, I was shocked and dismayed at how much my calf had shrunken in size. My muscle tone came back after a few weeks, but only after I did some strengthening exercises.

The Science of Exercise

Engaging in a regular exercise routine brings countless benefits. Being active strengthens and tones our muscles, maintains healthy bones, improves heart and lung function, reduces our risk of getting major diseases, and even stimulates the growth of new brain cells. According to a 2011 study published by the Mayo Clinic, working out may help to:

- Keep us young. Brisk walking or biking boosts the amount of oxygen taken in during exercise. Improving our aerobic capacity by only 15–25% would be like shaving 10–20 years off our age.
- Reduce infections. Even moderate workouts temporarily rev up the immune system by increasing the aggressiveness of immune cells. People who exercise generally catch fewer colds.
- Prevent heart attacks. Exercise not only raises "good" HDL cholesterol and lowers blood pressure, it reduces arterial inflammation, another risk factor for heart attacks and strokes.
- Ease asthma. New evidence shows that upper-body and breathing exercises can reduce the need to use an inhaler in mild cases of asthma.
- Control blood sugar. Regular brisk walking can significantly cut the risk of developing type 2 diabetes, as exercise helps to maintain a healthy blood-sugar level by increasing cells' sensitivity to insulin and by controlling weight.

- Protect against cancer. Exercise may reduce the risk of colon cancer by speeding waste through the stomach and lowering insulin levels. It may also protect against breast and prostate cancer by regulating hormone levels.
- Combat stress. Regular exercise lowers levels of stress hormones. For many, it helps relieve depression as effectively as antidepressant medication. Exercise releases hormones found in the brain, called endorphins, that create a sense of emotional and psychological well-being.
- Relieve hot flashes. Simple walking or practicing gentle yoga enhances mood and reduces some menopausal symptoms, such as hot flashes and night sweats.
- Prolong life. Studies lasting many years have consistently shown that being active cuts the risk of premature death by about 50% for men and women.

While the benefits of exercise cited above support long-term health and weight management, so many of us engage in exercise routines designed to make our bodies go away. We turn to exercise as another way to check out. This is similar to how chronic dieters use calorie restricting and counting as distractions from feelings they fear or the need not to feel. We push ourselves to commit to workout styles with which we may not be comfortable and that are not compatible with our personalities or body types. We exercise as a means to burn extra calories or the extra calories we imagine we consumed.

We are targets of media hype and are sucked in by celebrity trainers and reality TV shows that make us feel guilty for not spending hours in a gym. For example, in his book *The Calorie Myth*, Jonathan Bailor writes about Jay and Jennifer Jacobs, contestants on NBC's *Biggest Loser* who lost nearly 300 lbs. of combined weight. They admit that while they were thrilled with the results from dedicating every hour of their lives to extreme exercise, they needed to find a more sustainable approach in order to maintain happy and healthy lives.

A recent cover of *Seventeen Magazine* read, "Get an Insane Body." The caption read, "It's hard but you'll look hot."

Messages like these are extremely counterproductive, if not disheartening.

If we already have an unhealthy relationship with food and our bodies, these messages fuel the beliefs we develop about exercise. Exercising because we think we "have to" cheats us out of the pleasure we could have when our bodies move as they are inclined to. If we drag ourselves to the gym or shame ourselves into participating in activities we have no interest in, because we fear gaining weight or want to lose weight, we are living with a very toxic belief system that puts us into a stress response, which we know is counterproductive to the very thing we want to achieve. As stated previously, a stress response will cause our bodies to store fat, prevent fat loss, and decrease our ability to build lean muscle.

Over-exercising can cause fatigue and injury, which will end up sidelining us. It will take us away from time spent with friends and loved ones. It will perpetuate fears of hunger and appetite because it can cause cravings, especially if our diets are deficient in nutrients, a problem very often caused by the extreme dieting that is compelling us to over-exercise.

The flip side of telling ourselves we "have to" exercise is that doing so can cause the rebellious inner child in us to act out, making us avoid exercise in an attempt to prove who's in charge. Often we become overwhelmed, thinking we need to conquer weight and self-esteem issues before we can realize any benefits from an exercise routine. Either way, it's a no-win situation when exercise becomes another means of obsessing over the perfect body.

The saying "No pain, no gain" is outdated and inaccurate. We should not feel pain when we exercise. When we exercise for well-being, we are honoring the body we were given. We receive plentiful gains as we become empowered to take charge of our healthy lives. We find ourselves making better food choices and embracing a newfound energy that is both nourishing and nurturing.

When empowered and experiencing embodiment, we are filled with the sensations of being alive. We find ways to move that bring us pleasure versus punishment. When embodied, we can give up the scale—that dysfunctional piece of equipment whose only purpose is to keep us tied to dysfunctional thoughts about our bodies. The numbers we stay attached to grip us, rule us, and tell us when we can be happy. We don't have much of a chance to enjoy mindful eating or moving when we're focused on what the food we wish to eat will do to us or how the exercise we engage in will change us.

Clients often ask me about the best time of day to exercise and the best types of exercise. There are no right answers, other than the time and the type of movement that works best for you. I often counter with the question, "If every type of exercise burned the same amount of calories, what would you prefer to do?"

As some of us have more energy in the morning and others are more alert and focused in the evening, the time for us to work out should be dictated by our inner clocks. When we include our bodies in the conversation, we find out what suits us on any given day.

Different forms of exercise provide different types of energy. Just as there is no one right diet for everyone, and our diets may change with the seasons or as our needs change, our choice of movement can change.

Some of us are motivated by the camaraderie of team sports, some are inspired by a great fitness instructor in a class. Some of us prefer to exercise alone in the comfort of home, and some prefer being outdoors. The options are countless when we make pleasure and wellness the end goal.

Exercise can be the functional activities we perform as we go about our daily lives. Living in a city, I prefer to walk to my destinations, and I choose to take the stairs rather than an elevator or escalator when feasible. Cleaning house, carrying packages, walking the dog, and pushing your children or grandchildren in a stroller are all examples of functional exercise that don't require any special apparel or apparatus.

As with healthy eating, start with relaxation and compassion and open yourself to the possibility that you can be an active participant in this game of life. You can find pleasure in simple movement, moving with ease, confidence, and sensuality as you discover the most brilliant version of yourself.

Embrace It

- **Look in the mirror** and choose to love whoever stares back. Mirror work teaches us to develop a healthy perspective when we open ourselves up to the power of the positive by acknowledging all that is wonderful about the body we inhabit—for example, legs to carry us, arms to hug the ones we love, bellies that will or have carried our children.
- **Engage in physical activities you enjoy** rather than those you think you should be doing. Have a crazy dance party with yourself.
- **Make realistic, short-term goals** rather than statements such as, "I am going to run/walk three miles a day."
- **Convenience** should be a priority. Schedule time to work out that works well with your schedule and your body clock.
- **Give yourself the opportunity** to try something new. If the workout is challenging, try it again. Don't be intimidated because you may not get it right the first time.

Journal It

Do I exercise from a love of movement or because I fear I will gain weight if I don't?

_____

_____

_____

_____

_____

_____

_____

_____

_____

_____

_____

_____

_____

Affirm It

I take care of myself body, mind, and spirit, and in doing so, my outer beauty reflects my inner glow and lightness of being.

The number on a scale does not reflect my self-worth or how strong and healthy I am from within.

I can connect to all parts of my body as I connect to the power of movement.

I feel energized and further motivated when I exercise in a way that acknowledges my body's natural desire to move.

Although I may not always feel like exercising, knowing the benefits are important to my mind and spirit, I honor my body by moving.

CHAPTER 6

Only Eat Whole Foods (At Least As Often As You Can)

"Let food be thy medicine, let medicine be thy food."
—Hippocrates

I have counted calories and carb grams and restricted both. I have included protein at every meal and been careful to eat enough healthy fats. I have practiced veganism and vegetarianism, been pescatarian and nutritarian, gluten free, and dairy free. I have eaten my three square meals and smaller meals, 4–6 times a day. All of these practices boxed me in to a set of rules to follow, and if I deviated, I felt I had failed and blamed my lack of willpower.

This book is designed to end your war with food and inspire and motivate you toward experiencing and rejoicing in freedom with your food choices. I have shared suggestions and strategies for and the science behind reasons to adopt a relaxed attitude so you can ease into a lifestyle that allows you to enjoy food you love and connect to its energy, find a sense of serenity, and finally find peace with your body.

We fear food for many reasons. Some are founded in our stories, our histories. Some are founded in "toxic nutritional beliefs," a term coined by Marc David, founder of the Institute for the Psychology of Eating. Some are based on being told by the experts, such as doctors, celebrity chefs, and actors turned nutritionists and lifestyle gurus, that we should eat this, not that.

My sincere hope is that you come away from this chapter with a renewed understanding of both the nutritional and spiritual properties of the food you eat. I also hope you will have the curiosity and desire to explore different types of foods and dietary systems in an effort to discover what is most beneficial for you.

Following the latest trends and hanging on to the words of someone whose body type may be unreasonable for you to emulate will only set you up for disappointment. While some dietary practices are well-suited for me regarding how satisfied I am, my energy level, productivity, glowing skin, and weight, the same may not be true for you. That is the lesson of bio-individuality: there is no one right diet for everybody. Diets are not generic, nor does one size fit all.

While this chapter will enlighten you about the benefits of a balanced diet, I encourage you to experiment with what feels best for you. Pay attention to the days you have more or less energy, note what foods you ate, then adjust your diet accordingly by eating more or less protein, carbohydrates, and healthy fats.

We are biologically individual; we have different characteristics that will dictate what our bodies need. Our genetics play a role, and many experts in the field of nutrition believe our blood types do too. Overall wellness, stress, age, and activity level all play a part. Seasons of the year and accompanying climate changes can influence what our bodies need too. For example, extremely hot climates will call for more carbohydrates than fat, while colder climates will create the need for more protein and fat so we can say warmer.

As you ease into including your body in the conversation and learn who you want to be when you sit down at the table, you'll feel empowered as you choose foods to energize you, satisfy you, and yes, bring you pleasure.

In a perfect world, we would all be eating fresh, organic, seasonal, and whole food. Our meals would consist of nutrient-dense plant foods and proteins, unrefined grains, whole fruits, and healthy fats. I know this is not always possible because we travel, enjoy having meals in restaurants, and get caught up in the fast pace of our home and work lives, not to mention because of the cost and availability of some of these foods.

The Standard American Diet, referred to by many as SAD, has become a cause of disease while obesity levels are the highest in history. Americans rely on a diet that is the most highly processed and refined of any in the world.

What follows are explanations of essential nutrients and some well-publicized and simple dietary theories surrounding them.

Calories

I start here because a common misconception is that if we simply eat fewer calories than our bodies require, we will lose weight. The "calories in/calories out" theory has been floating around for decades. I am happy to report it is old science. We know that calories are substances that produce heat, and heat produces energy that fuels our bodies. This energy allows us to function physically, emotionally, and psychologically. We also know that all calories are not created equal and that the quality of the calories we take in will have a positive or negative effect on the way we expend the energy, i.e. metabolism. For example, one hundred calories of vegetables or high-quality protein or fat is going to be more valuable to the body than a one-hundred-calorie snack pack, commercially produced and comprised of refined carbohydrates.

In *The Calorie Myth*, Jonathan Bailor addresses this in detail, citing 1,200 studies. He points out that when we choose from foods that are plant-based, nutrient-dense proteins, fats from whole foods, and low-sugar fruits, to managing our weight is effortless and we are able to consume more food than we imagined we could.

Whole Foods

Whole foods are those that are not changed in any way from the time they are harvested until the time we purchase them. Whole foods are abundant in the nutrients, vitamins, and minerals we are able to digest and assimilate into the proteins, carbohydrates, and fats we use for energy.

Examples of whole foods are proteins such as meat, fish, poultry, and eggs; fat sources including avocados, nuts, and seeds; carbohydrate sources comprised of fresh vegetables and fruits, whole grains, herbs, and seed vegetables.

Sometimes, whole foods need to be changed from their natural state to be consumed. An example would be peeling an orange or cooking whole grains or beans. These examples are about food needing to be digestible and palatable. The difference between whole foods and nonwhole foods is in how much the food was chemically altered and processed. If we make these foods the foundation of our diets, we improve our immunity, enjoy greater physical and mental energy and better digestion, and will have leaner bodies. Our bodies were designed to eat such foods; therefore, they metabolize thee foods the most efficiently.

Does it make sense to avoid certain whole fruits and vegetables because they may be higher in sugar, yet rely on processed protein bars for our nutrition in an effort to shed pounds?

Fresh Foods

Fresh food is alive and full of nutrients. From the time a food is harvested, it begins to lose valuable nutrients. The longer getting food from the field to your table takes, the more vitamins, minerals, and enzymes are lost.

A huge distribution network operates to get food from the fields to the superstores and markets we rely on. Food is harvested, then delivered on trucks to distribution centers where it is shipped to local stores or even other countries before being trucked again to the market.

From there, the food is warehoused until it is rotated out for sale in the appropriate section of the store. The freshest produce will be placed in the bottom of the bins, and the fresher milk, eggs, and meats will be placed to the back of the refrigerator in an effort to sell the food that has been there first. We buy the food, take it home, and maybe put it in the refrigerator for a few days. Our food could be weeks old by the time we eat it.

Since many of us are not inclined to grow our own produce or raise chickens for eggs, we need to be aware of where our food is coming from. I recommend choosing food from local farmers when possible. Modern farming and agricultural techniques have created big business for corporations involved in the processing and delivery of food, which doesn't translate into good nutrition.

One way to stay true to the concept of supporting local farmers and insuring the nutrient value of our food is to eat vegetables and fruits in season. In fall and winter, eat apples from New York or Washington State. In the warmer months, enjoy peaches from Georgia, tomatoes from New Jersey or those farmed close to where you live. Fruit and vegetables from South America had to travel a long way over a large amount of time to be delivered to your local store.

Seasonal Foods

Choosing and eating foods that are in harmony with the season we are experiencing not only affords us the benefits of fresh food, but will help us adapt to the change of season and accompanying climate changes. If you live in a region where the winters are very cold, very little fresh produce will be available from local sources. In this case, it's best to eat nurturing and warming foods like soups, grains, and root vegetables.

As spring arrives, fruits and greens that create a more cooling effect in our bodies will become more abundant and help clear some of the accumulated waste we've stored in our bodies through the winter months when we are less active in the fresh outdoors and eating heavier foods.

Summer brings the most variety of cooling foods, which contain more moisture. Juicier fruits like grapes, melons, and berries, along with lettuces and tomatoes help our bodies cope with the hottest temperatures of the year by keeping us hydrated.

People who live in climates with less of a seasonal change will have different choices, but there will still be foods specific to the season.

We can find berries in New York during the winter months, but keep in mind they are most likely coming from far away. The vital nutrients in plant foods that protect us from disease and ensure our health are lost when these foods are picked before they are ripe so they won't spoil when shipped long distances. Along with the health benefits of fresh-grown produce, seasonal foods are far more cost-effective. It is very expensive to ship food around the globe.

Nutrition 101

We are what we eat, and our level of energy and overall wellness will reflect this fact. Nutrition is where the food meets the body. A nutrient-rich diet ensures we'll have physical and mental energy, while a diet deficient in nutrients will rob our bodies of such energy. The consequences will be fatigue, low energy, poor muscle tone, dry skin, hair, and nails, low libido, often weight gain, and an environment for disease to set in.

Let's start with a simple explanation of macronutrients. Here I will briefly describe the types and characteristics of each, giving you insight into their benefits and how deficiencies in each can become symptomatic.

Protein

Protein supplies the building blocks for the cells and structures in our bodies. This makes protein an essential part of every one of our billions of cells. While most foods contain protein, the higher the percentage of protein, the greater the ability to build up the body. This is due to the amount of amino acids in protein-rich foods, amino acids being what make up protein. Meat, poultry, fish, eggs, dairy foods, nuts, and seeds have higher concentrations of these amino acids and therefore a higher percentage of cell-building protein.

While plants and grains contain some amino acids, they provide less than the foods listed above. I am not indicating that one type is better than the other, just pointing out the difference between protein sources.

High-quality proteins are found in organic meats and poultry, wild and conscientiously raised fish and seafood, whole-soy foods, organic dairy products, free-range, organic eggs, and organic nuts and seeds.

Poor-quality proteins include commercially processed soy protein, factory-farmed meat and poultry, and processed deli-meats.

Symptoms of protein deficiencies are commonly seen in individuals who chronically diet and restrict calories or follow extreme vegetarian or vegan diets. They can include:

- irritability
- fatigue
- low energy
- poor memory
- poor attention span
- moodiness
- cravings and hunger
- hair loss
- brittle hair and nails
- poor digestion
- poor circulation
- feeling cold
- poor muscle tone
- sleep issues
- slow wound healing
- low sex drive

How much protein do we need? As individuals, our needs differ. During times of growth such as childhood or pregnancy, our need for protein is greater. Recovery from surgery or an illness requires more protein, Athletes, people who are more active, and even children who need help focusing attention will benefit from including concentrated sources of protein into their regular diets.

As stated in previous paragraphs, our needs for protein can change as the seasons do in an effort to sync our bodies to their immediate environment.

Some examples of popular diet and lifestyle choices that promote the majority of macronutrients come from protein are the Paleo Diet, the Atkins Diet and the Dukan Diet. While each of these programs is backed up by theory and science, they may not resonate with you.

Many followers of the Paleo Diet are convinced we should eat as our hunter-gatherer ancestors did. While very popular, this diet restricts natural grains and certain fruits, claiming these carbohydrate sources could be at the root of disease and weight gain. Our ancestors weren't drinking super-sized sodas or scarfing down overly processed foods and commercially baked goods, either.

The Atkins Diet has us counting carb grams and starts with two weeks of minimal consumption. No tomatoes or carrots, but cheeseburgers, fried eggs, and bacon. How many people do you know who put weight on because they included tomatoes and carrots in their diets?

The Dukan Diet originated in France and gained popularity when it was publicized as the diet of choice by Kate Middleton and her family before her wedding to Prince Charles. This diet also relies on protein, and allows you to have vegetables and oat bran, but one day a week is dedicated to eating only protein. The diet is divided into four phases. The first is the Attack Phase ...

Carbohydrates

Carbohydrates are an essential macronutrient, providing energy that fuels our bodies and our brains minute by minute, whether awake or asleep. Our internal organs, nervous system, and muscles depend on carbohydrates in order to function. They help us metabolize protein and fat and contain the fiber, sugars, starches, vitamins, minerals, and enzymes we need for optimal health and well-being. They are reliable sources of nutrition and sustainable energy.

Carbohydrates encompass a wide range of foods. All of the sweeteners we know, real or artificial, are carbohydrates. All fruits are carbohydrates. All vegetables from leafy greens to crunchy red peppers are carbohydrates. Most plant sources of food are carbohydrate, even though they may contain some protein and fat. Legumes including beans and peas, and all grains, whether they are refined or not, are carbohydrates. Alcohol is also a carbohydrate, in a very reduced form.

While in their natural form, carbohydrates are essential to the body, but the overly processed and refined carbohydrates we have in abundance offer no nutritional benefits and are, in fact, depleting. This means that they don't provide the body with nutritive value when we eat them, so our bodies take energy from stored sources in order to thrive.

Carbohydrates have gotten a bad reputation in many circles, and a lot of dieters feel if they avoid carbs they will be thin. Truth be told, without some amount of carbohydrates we wouldn't be able to function. It is the quality—there is that word again—of the carbohydrates that matters to our health and our waistlines.

Carbohydrate needs differ greatly from one person to another. To figure out what is right for you, experiment and listen to your body rather than the latest diet or weight-loss fad.

The best sources of carbohydrates are plant foods like vegetables and fruits. Some of these have more concentrated sugars and are digested better by some people than others. Beans, lentils, and other legumes are high-quality carbohydrates. Whole grains are a valuable source of fiber, vitamins, minerals, and enzymes.

Have you or are you thinking of adopting a gluten-free diet? It's become a craze that has taken over our book and supermarket shelves. Gluten is the protein found in wheat. Some people are unable to digest this protein and actually suffer from an autoimmune illness called celiac disease. This can make you very uncomfortable and result in malabsorption of nutrients and other serious complications. Others are just sensitive to gluten, suffering with symptoms after eating it that can include a variety of digestive issues and low thyroid function.

Many nutrition theorists believe today's wheat does not resemble the wheat we were predesigned to digest, as it is treated in an effort to increase production. If you suspect you are gluten sensitive, eliminate it from your diet for several weeks. Then reintroduce it and see how you feel. If you suspect you may have celiac disease, see your doctor for a simple blood test.

The carbohydrates of poor quality are high fructose corn syrup, white flour products, corn flour products, and commercial cereals, breads, pastries, and soft drinks. Reliance on these sources of carbohydrates can act as a cause for:

- weight gain
- cravings and hunger
- nutrient depletion
- unhealthy blood cholesterol levels
- blood sugar and insulin destabilization
- fatty liver
- heart disease
- dementia

Vegan, vegetarian, and raw food diets rely on plant-based foods for sustenance. Vegans include no dairy or eggs in their diets, and many followers of this lifestyle avoid wearing or using products made with substances derived from any type of animal.

Vegetarian lifestyles can be more flexible in that some who practice them eat eggs and dairy. Raw-food enthusiasts eat plants, nuts, and seeds and nothing that is heated above 135 degrees, believing doing so robs food of necessary enzymes. Some follow these lifestyles for humanitarian reasons as well as believing in the health benefits of such diets. A problem arises when the sources of carbohydrates are refined and processed or if the body requires more protein for reasons stated above.

On the other hand, one can be carbohydrate deficient and suffer from

- cravings for carbohydrates (Unfortunately, these cravings often show up as craving the poor quality carbs)
- digestive issues which show up as constipation due to a lack of fiber
- lack of energy
- nausea
- headache
- halitosis; and/or
- nutritional deficiencies in minerals and B-vitamins.

Fat

Fat is not the evil menace it has been often made out to be. It is an essential macronutrient, just as vital to our health and well-being as protein and carbohydrates. Fats play several important roles in our bodies. They are an essential element of our cell membranes and provide protection for our internal organs. Fats help to regulate our body temperature and blood-sugar levels and provide insulation for our nerves. Essential fatty acids (EFAs) are the building blocks of hormones, cell walls, the brain, and hundreds of different chemicals that continually impact metabolism. They supply energy and facilitate the absorption of the fat-soluble vitamins A, D, E, and K. These vitamins are abundant in the greens and vegetables we rely on to make beautiful salads. When we restrict fat by using fat-free dressings in an effort to save calories, our salads become a wasteland of nutrition.

Fat gives us a sense of fullness and satiety. It sustains us because it takes longest to digest and metabolize. It gives us a sense of warmth and nourishment, eliciting a pleasure response.

In the late 1970s, prominent scientists believed that saturated fat, the fat found in animal products and some whole-plant foods, was the main cause of heart disease because it raised LDL cholesterol (bad cholesterol) in the blood. This was the impetus of the low-fat diet craze that was highly recommended to Americans. However not a single study on this diet was done at the time, so the American public became participants in the largest uncontrolled experiment in history. This experiment didn't turn out so well, and we are suffering the consequences today, as the obesity epidemic started at the same time, followed by the diabetes epidemic. The problem was that we stopped eating meat and eggs and started turning to processed and refined carbohydrates. Subsequent studies showed people on low-fat diets lost an insignificant amount of weight in comparison with control groups on normal diets.(2)

Research since then has shown that cholesterol in our food does not raise cholesterol in the blood. Eggs, for example, are a powerhouse of nutrition and will actually raise the good cholesterol, HDL, providing us with protein, vitamins, minerals, and powerful nutrients like lutein and choline that are essential for the health of our eyes and our brains.

Avoiding fat because you fear it will end up on your body is reacting to an irrational and inaccurate belief. How we view fat varies from culture to culture. The French love it, Native Americans revere it, and Americans love it, hate it, and fear it all at the same time. The fat you store on your body depends on the type and quality of fat you consume, not the amount. While fat is essential to our health and metabolism, all fat is not created equal.

High-quality fats will contribute to better health and weight loss while poor-quality fats promote symptoms that create weight gain. As in most nutritional research, studies exist that claim validity for both sides, those in favor of a diet which includes sources of full fat and those which limit fat. What we do know is that there are good, healthy fats which are healing to the body.

Examples of healthy fats are oils such as olive, sesame, coconut, sunflower, and flax; olives, avocados, wild fish, free-range, organic eggs, raw nuts and seeds, and raw coconuts.

Fat deficiency, in the form of a lack of essential fatty acids, can create symptoms that include:

- poor digestion
- fatigue, irritability, and moodiness
- constipation
- dry skin, hair, and nails
- redness around the eyes
- hunger
- stiff or painful joints
- thirst
- poor memory
- difficulty losing weight

We want to avoid fats that are overly heated or exposed to hydrogen. These are the trans fats that are prevalent in most commercially baked goods. Manufacturers love trans fats because they extend the shelf life of the products. The problem is that the body has a hard time metabolizing and clearing them, so they tend to accumulate and cause plaque buildup at the cellular level.

Some researchers, like Weston Price, teach that saturated fat in dairy is not only harmless but beneficial. Others—for example, Mark Hyman—believe these same fats have a dangerous effect on LDL, our bad cholesterol.

This is where moderation and bio-individuality must prevail. However, the experts are in agreement that the ideas that low fat means healthy and that low fat is good for weight loss are outdated science.

An example of a lifestyle where healthy fat plays a role is the Mediterranean diet. This way of eating emphasizes vegetables, whole grains, lean proteins and fat from olive oil, nuts, and seeds.

Water

We can survive for a month without food but only a few days without water. Water is considered an essential part of a healthy diet. Our bodies are 75% water, and we must continually put back what is lost through activity and the simple functioning of our daily routines.

When considering your water intake each day, take into account the water content of your food choices. Fruits and vegetables are high in water content while breads and cereals are not. Herbal tea, soup, and juice will count toward your water intake, but caffeinated beverages like coffee, tea, and soda actually dehydrate the body.

Not drinking enough water can cause symptoms of low energy and cravings that can be mistaken as hunger. A good rule of thumb for how much water you should drink in a day is to consume half your body weight in ounces. For example, a 150 lb person should have seventy-five ounces of water. This should increase if you are exercising or visiting a hot climate.

The Energetics of Food

We should not only value food for its nutrition but for the experience it gives us and the energy it creates in our bodies. If "you are what you eat," and food impacts our bodies on a cellular level, consider how it may impact our relationship to life. While you are becoming aware of the diversity and properties of the food you consume, consider that each food has its own unique energy. What if we assimilate not only the nutrients but the energy of the food we eat? In his book, *The Energetics of Food: Encounters with Your Most Intimate Relationships*, Steven Gagne explains that foods have their own distinct characteristics. He teaches that where foods come from and how they grow affect the energy they provide.

For example, plant foods such as greens reach toward the sun, soaking up the chlorophyll. Eating such foods provides our blood with oxygen and therefore lifts our spirits, helping us to feel lighter. Other vegetables like squash grow close to the ground and are mood balancing. Root vegetables, which grown downward into the ground, have a strong energy to ground us when we feel overstimulated.

There is also a strong connection between food and mood. Some meal choices will make us feel dull and sluggish while others will raise our spirits and energy levels.

Science tells us that the food–mood phenomenon happens because of brain chemicals called *neurotransmitters*. These are chemical messengers that relay actions throughout the brain. Examples of these neurotransmitters are serotonin, which makes us feel relaxed, and dopamine and norepinephrine, which are stimulating.

Eating carbohydrate-rich foods releases serotonin, which will make us feel relaxed, but overdoing the carbs will create drowsiness. A protein-rich meal will release the dopamine and norepinephrine, causing us to feel alert and focused. In this case, overdoing the protein will cause us to feel tense and irritable. Again, each of us will have a different reaction to food and mood. Only you can know the right amounts of protein, carbohydrates, and fat you need in order to achieve the feelings of health and well-being you desire.

As we step closer toward food freedom, incorporate these techniques and strategies into our daily routines and mindset, experience and appreciate a newfound energy, we will start to realize that feeling otherwise just doesn't make any sense.

Embrace It

- **Experiment** with which type of diet makes you feel best. Spend a few days eating more protein or less, more good-quality carbohydrates or less, or more high-quality fats or less. Record how you feel right after you eat and again two hours later. Track your mood and your energy level.
- **Conduct a Breakfast experiment.** For seven days enjoy a different breakfast. Again, note how you feel after you eat and again two hours later.

Day 1: Scrambled eggs or omelette with vegetable
Day 2: Greek yogurt or cottage cheese and fruit
Day 3: Oatmeal
Day 4: Commercially boxed breakfast cereal
Day 5: Muffin and coffee
Day 6: Fresh fruit smoothie
Day 7: Fresh vegetables and hummus

Journal It

What are the nutritional and diet beliefs you feel most strongly about, and how do you imagine they can change?

_____

_____

_____

_____

_____

_____

_____

_____

_____

_____

_____

_____

_____

Affirm It

Healthy eating and I are one, and I am richly rewarded as this way of living is becoming easy and fun for me

I let go of all reasons and excuses for not eating healthy meals.

I replace dieting with healthy eating principles and habits.

Eating healthy foods makes me look and feel better, while feelings of confidence and comfort come from my thoughts, not food.

The universe offers me an abundance of wonderfully nourishing food, and I am so very grateful.

Read More about It

Marc Hyman, *The Ultra Metabolism Diet*, New York, Atria Books, Simon and Schuster, 2006

Joshua Rosenthal, *Integrative Nutrition*, Texas, Greenleaf Book Group, 2007

Julia Ross, *The Mood Cure: The 4 Step Program to Re-balance Your Natural Sense of Well-Being,* New York, Penguin Group, 2002

Steve Gagne, *Energetics of Food: Encounters with Your Most Intimate Connection*, Vermont, Healing Arts Press, 2006

CHAPTER 7

Make Sure You Are Surrounded By What Truly Nourishes

For so much of my life, I thought I could handle all I had to by myself. I was never comfortable asking for help or advice. This did not serve me well, for it made for a very lonely existence, especially when I needed nourishment the most. I know this now as I review the last ten years of my journey.

Losing my husband when I was forty-nine threw me into a tailspin. Not only was I faced with my own grief and confusion, but my daughters had also suffered a devastating loss.

I had the business of my life to deal with and relationships to navigate. I was floundering in a sea of uncertainty, and instead of reaching for a life ring to pull me in, I resorted to a monologue of clichés and retreated into a cycle of addictive behaviors: food restricting and compulsive eating, lavish spending, and social drinking that became abusive.

The concept of self-nourishment was foreign to me as I never associated it with how to take care of myself.

Relationships slipped away as I retreated into a dark place. I let go of wonderful women who wanted to support and love me. I was overwhelmed and disassociated from life as I knew it. Unsure how to create a new normal for myself, my immediate reaction was to isolate and retreat to a space of my own. I became defensive as I protected myself against what hurt so badly. That very protective instinct actually reinforced the walls I was building and only served to isolate and separate me further from the world and healing.

I had no concept of developing a spiritual muscle that would teach me something greater than myself existed. I didn't know I could find it if I opened up to letting go of the fear that kept me wrapped up in my small world.

My work was coming from a disingenuous place as I was disconnected from my authenticity. Not being nourished by movement, I needed to learn that appropriate and healthy exercise could connect me to my body's higher wisdom.

My journey back home to myself opened my eyes to the amazing possibilities that occur when we leave fear-based life behind and unlock the door to love, acceptance, and compassion. The journey stopped being about loss and became about embracing what's available to me now.

With that realization came the reality that there comes a time to respectfully and lovingly let go of what has reached its rightful end. Seeing this freed me to change. The newly claimed knowledge that I am enough allows me to face uncertainty and rely on myself in a different way. Accepting my humanness and imperfection allows me to handle the strength of my emotions so I can live in balance as opposed to extremes.

I use my voice to translate my needs and desires into words. I thrive on curiosity and engage in new relationships without judgment or expectation as I receive the gifts of the universe.

To be nourished is to be sustained with food; to have supplied your body with what is necessary for life, health, and growth; to be cherished, fostered, kept alive; to be strengthened, built up, or promoted.

We are nourished by so much more than the food we put on our plates, or eat while standing in front of the refrigerator, in our beds, or while on the computer. In order to feel the completeness and satisfaction of a well-fed soul, we need to address the areas of our lives that feed and sustain us. We need to be in our lives as active participants rather than losing ourselves to surviving. When what truly nourishes us is abundant, life feeds us.

By now you may have figured out that having a healthy relationship with food and your body is not so much about *what* you eat, but about *who you are as an eater*. It's less about nutrition and more about nourishment. Because when you are nourished in your life, it's *so* much easier to have a positive relationship with food.

Nourishment is not only nutrition, but the experience of that nutrition; the heartiness and the sentiment behind what the meal brings to you. It's the difference between participating with wonder and joy or with confusion and uncertainty. It's the difference between eating with pleasure rather than for pleasure. It's the difference between eating with emotion rather than eating so as not to feel emotion. Our relationship with food can bring us theories and disputes, pain and aliveness, but always the knowledge that we can always return for more.

In our busy world with its emphasis on responsibility, work, child rearing, and staying connected, to be healthy and balanced we must focus on more than just our bodies; we must feed our hearts, minds, and spirits.

Have you noticed that when your body, mind, and spirit are engaged in a creative project or happy relationship, your reliance on food seems to decrease? Being passionately in love or involved in an exciting project creates feelings of exhilaration that fuel us.

Likewise, when you are unsatisfied with your relationships, your job, or other areas of your life, you may depend on food to cheer, soothe, or sedate you. When your life is out of balance, no amount of food can feed you where you truly need nourishment. The food we eat is very important for health and balance, but what really feeds us, a full and fulfilling life, is not served on a plate.

What Are You Hungry For?

Our entire reality and how we take care of ourselves
is based on our sense of self. This includes the
quality of our intention and attention to all matters.
Health comes from connection. The origins of the
word health come from the word whole. Health is
wholeness, and when our sense of self is whole, we
can finally achieve good health.

—Deepak Chopra MD.

Healthy relationships, fulfilling life choices, regular and enjoyable
movement, and a spiritual connection all serve to feed us and help us
feel nourished and nurtured. The thousands of moments that make
up our life experience fuel us mentally, emotionally, physically, and
spiritually. We hunger for essential elements as love, connection,
touch, success, adventure, joy, and self-expression.

Being able to recognize our need for these elements and be
able to incorporate them into our lives determines how full and
rewarding our lives feel. When we use food as a means to satisfy
our hunger for what we emotionally or spiritually need, our bodies
and minds suffer.

The most important and fundamental relationship is the one we
have with ourselves. That relationship will affect all others, whether
with family, friends, partners, or coworkers. Our issues with weight
have become an illustration of unavailability on some level. For
whatever reason that is unique to each of us, we have felt alone and
on the outside, put a wall up, and then felt even more alone, and for
many of us, shame about where our behavior has taken us.

Whether our issue came from fear-based living or not feeling
enough, it is important to know that until we open up to the
possibility of receiving nourishment from relationships in our lives,
it is hard to find lasting freedom with food.

Disordered eating and compulsive behaviors with food, whether
restricting or binging, cause us to isolate. In that place of aloneness,
it becomes easy to self-destruct as the voice that tells us we need to

indulge in our strongest craving becomes louder than our expression of our true self, which in reality craves human connection.

Being alone is radically different from isolating. It's essential to be aware of the difference. Cultivating a peaceful space within our selves provides us a safe and sacred home to continually return to, whereas when we isolate, we build walls around ourselves in order to conduct negative self-talk.

Connecting to our selves in splendid solitude is the true gift of nourishment. Choosing to be alone by denying relationships forces us into a prison of isolation. It is a trap and an illusion. In isolation, we are with the darkness of our compulsive behavior. Increased distance from friends and loved ones brings a darker connection to food, as it calls to us, accepting and making us feel better, if only for a brief time.

Reaching out to others in a way that connects us compassionately is extremely nourishing. It is an integral part of the healing process that leads us to the path of freedom as we transform our relationship with food.

An equally integral part is learning to receive the gifts of the universe. In our darkness, we reject the bounty of abundance offered by people, places, and things because we feel unworthy or mistrustful. Sometimes we are waiting for conditions to be met before we accept these gifts, like losing weight or being in better shape. Being open and allowing ourselves to be vulnerable makes us human and attracts an audience that will feed our needs for the light-filled life we are seeking. When we are willing to receive, the goodness we hunger for has its rightful home.

Clear the Clutter

Don't wait for spring to clean up and clear the clutter. Look around you and decide what things you are dealing with no longer serve you. Just as we no longer need to hold on to outdated and worn-out clothing, we no longer need to hold on to toxic relationships and unrealistic dreams.

While you are at it, don't forget to clear your heart. Throw away the negative thoughts and attachment to the story you've been holding on to just because it's what you know. Be curious—are these habits and beliefs serving a purpose? A clean, open heart will allow you to receive all the good that awaits you each and every day. Just like rooms in your house, a cluttered heart and mind have no room for the new gifts and surprises that life will offer.

Cherished memories remain in our hearts and minds forever, if we are fortunate, but objects do not define us. Painful memories can serve to teach meaningful lessons but only if we clear the way for healing. Letting go of the stuff allows us to bid farewell to the past and receive the new energy of a happy, healthy future.

Is Your Definition of Success Nourishing or Eating at You?

In today's society, many of us spend most of the hours of our day working to better our station in life, making more money and feel more powerful. The paradox is that while we are seeking power, we risk losing ourselves to ambition.

A direct correlation exists between satisfaction or lack of it in our work lives and our behavior with food. Are you stressed during the day and not taking a proper lunch break, finding yourself grabbing cookies or candy from a coworker's desk? Do you come home feeling unappreciated and spent, finding yourself checking out with your biggest meal of the day and following it with a pint of ice cream? Workplace stress has been linked to faster aging, high blood pressure, and depression. A majority of us don't use our allotted vacation time, and eight out of ten of us are stressed about our jobs.

I want to share some insight from an article reporting that many Americans are revisiting this way of thinking and living. They are discovering that success can be measured in many different ways. The article goes on to describe what the author refers to as the Third Metric.(1)

The old definition of success blends money with power. This third metric implies a new definition where the circle of life is completed by what we need to embrace for a new way of thinking— health, mindfulness, friendship, passion, sleep, family, giving back, wisdom, empathy, and lastly, money and power. The article concludes with the thought that today's definition of a successful life includes the acceptance of detours along the way.

As we realize the importance for money and financial responsibility in our lives, it is important to keep a healthy perspective on the quality of our lives. Authenticity, paying it forward, regularly assessing our hunger for power and success, and taking time to be aware of what motivates us will keep the scales of work/life balance in check.

Spiritual Awareness Nourishes

All through this book I have made direct and indirect reference to the importance of awareness in our lives. Awareness for the blessings, awareness for the thoughts that become beliefs, awareness for what is true, awareness of our hunger and what we are hungry for, awareness for who we are at the table, and awareness of the wisdom of our bodies. While thoughts are only thoughts, awareness lets us acknowledge our thoughts and feelings without letting them define us. When we do this, we find hope and manifest our most desired goals.

Chances are if you are reading this book, you have awareness that you are dealing with issues that once addressed, can bring about lasting change. This is the first step to transformation. Without such awareness, we remain stagnant with a strong guarantee we won't experience growth. Awareness allows us to gain clarity and direction.

We arrive at this part of the journey ready to claim our freedom, already whole. However, after so many years of building layers of protection, we forget who we are beneath that surface. Awareness connects us to our core as it aligns us with the circle of life that brings peace and nourishment. From that center, we find a spiritual connection that when tapped, keeps us present and free, for we know life is just as it should be.

For some, that spiritual connection is with a tangible God; for some, it is a universal life force. Whatever it may be for you, awareness of and connection to your deepest self transcends you to your highest self, your higher power. In this place, we let go of self-doubt and judgment as we become empowered and open to wondrous possibilities.

Even when we are scared and disappointed, when faced with grief, sadness, confusion, and personal drama, we can change our relationship to what has happened and positively affect our experience. The value of this experience with the dark night of the soul is that we learn to set boundaries, make conscious choices, and practice integrity as we are continually empowered to move through life without fear.

Empowered awareness allows us to transform habits that may or may not be serving us. With it, are free to let go and relax into the uncertainty that continues to abound, but this time with faith. With empowered awareness we can make changes we otherwise hesitated on. We learn that unless we change what we do, we won't change what we get, and we can embrace the un-doing that change fosters.

Renew and rejoice in your relationship with food now. A healthy relationship with food is a healthy relationship with life. A healthy appetite for food and for life must be honored as a basic act of love. Feed that hunger rather than fear it and embrace a truly nourished and extraordinary journey. This is where the healing happens.

Embrace It

- **Everyday, make a commitment to consume something positive.** Find a teacher, mentor, book, blog, or community that inspires and uplifts you. Even if it's a few words of inspiration each day, you literally are what you "eat."
- Make a list, mentally or in your journal, of things you can do to **reach out** and increase your connection to others.
- Compile a **pleasure inventory.** List every thing, every person, and every place you can connect to pleasure. What or who on this list can you bring into your daily life?

Journal It

What does freedom look like for me, and what do I need to let go of in order to have it?

_____

_____

_____

_____

_____

_____

_____

_____

_____

_____

_____

_____

_____

_____

_____

Affirm It

As I give my concerns, fears, and worries to the universe, all of my needs are met miraculously, peacefully, quickly, and gracefully.

Read More about It

Thomas Moore, *The Dark Night of the Soul: A Guide to Finding Your Way Through Life's Ordeals*, USA,Gotham Books, Penguin Group, 2005

Marc David, *Nourishing Wisdom,* New York, Bell Tower, Harmony Books, 1991

Pia Chodrun, *Comfortable With Uncertainty: 108 Teachings on Cultivating Fearlessness and Compassion*, Boston, Shambhala Publications, 2003

Marianne Williamson, *A Course in Weightloss*: 21 Spiritual Lessons For surrendering Your Weight Forever, USA, Hay House, 2010

FINAL THOUGHTS

As this guide to food freedom concludes, it is really a beginning for you to stay on the course to developing a new and joyful relationship with food.

We have covered a lot, but it is essential to remember that the foundation to a healthy relationship with food is built on practicing gratitude to taste what we have and let go of our attachment to the stories that no longer serve us.

We've learned to question and experience our feelings, even when they are uncomfortable. We have learned to honor physical hunger and appreciate rather than reject our appetites because appetite is our life force.

We've seen the importance of slowing down and being mindful, and we've discovered the gift of body wisdom as opposed to wishing our bodies away. Lastly, we can find personal nourishment from things other than food.

I won't deceive you by promising that this path is not littered with obstacles. For many of us, our behavior with food has served a meaningful purpose in that it kept us somewhere we felt safe.

As life happens, sometimes unpredictably, we may feel pulled back. We may revert to old behaviors of overeating or restricting. If so, remember to breathe. Conscious breathing will put you into a state of presence and relaxation.

Know you can feel empowered to disengage from the old voice of negativity, and you can do so again and again, as needed, until it becomes a new normal. You'll find your sacred space where the compassion, acceptance, and forgiving happens.

Be gentle with yourself as you meet your emotions and give them the freedom to be so they can clear out, ensuring they don't stay longer than they need to.

To be continued ...

BIBLIOGRAPHY/ RESOURCES

Chapter 1

(1) Journal of Personality and Social Psychology, Michael E. Mc Cullogh and Robert A. Emmons, 2003
(2) American Psychologist, Martin Seligman, Tracy A. Steen, Nansoon Park, and Christopher Peterson, 2005
Mary O'Malley, *The Gift of our Compulsions,* California, New World Library, 2004
Geneen Roth, *Women, Food and God,* New York, Scribner, 2010
Byron Katie and Steven Mitchell, *Loving What is,* New York, Three Rivers press, 2002
Hale Dwoskin and Jack Canfield, *The Sedona Method*: Your key to Lasting Happiness, Success, Peace and Emotional Well-Being, Sedona, Sedona Press, 2007

Chapter 2

(1) P. Bjorntorp, "Psychosocial Factors and Fat Distribution," obesity in Europe '91,
(2) B.G. Lipinski, "Life Change Events as Correlates of Weight Gain," *Recent Advances in Obesity Research*, 1975.
(3) The Role of Resilience in Recovery, Gurze Books
Marc David, *The Slow Down Diet: Eating for Pleasure, Energy and Weight Loss*, Healing Arts Press, 2005
Mark Hyman, *The Ultra Mind Solution*, USA, Simon and Schuster, 2009

Chapter 3

Geneen Roth, When Food Is Love, New York, Plume, The Penguin Group, 1992

Evelyn Tribole and Elyse Resch, *Intuitive Eating*, New York, St. Martin's Griffin, 1995

Karen Koenig, *Rules of Normal Eaters: A Commonsense Approach for Dieters, Overeaters, Undereaters, Emotional Eaters, and Everyone In Between*, California, Gurze Books, 2005

Marc David, *Nourishing Wisdom*, New York, Bell Tower, Harmony Books, 1991

Chapter 4

(1) S.G.R.Barclay, "Effect of the Psychosocial Stress on Salt and Water Transport in the Human jejunum, Gastroenterology 93, no.1(July 1987)

Marc David, *The Slow Down Diet: Eating for Pleasure, Energy and Weight Loss*, Vermont, Healing Arts Press, 2005

Chapter 6

(1) www.businessinsider.com/9 lies about health that destroyed the world's health, 2013-11

(2) Women's Health Initiative

Marc Hyman, *The Ultra Metabolism Diet*, New York, Atria Books, Simon and Schuster, 2006

Joshua Rosenthal, *Integrative Nutrition*, Texas, Greenleaf Book Group, 2007

Julia Ross, *The Mood Cure: The 4 Step Program to Re-balance Your Natural Sense of Well-Being*, New York, Penguin Group, 2002

Steve Gagne, *Energetics of Food: Encounters with Your Most Intimate Connection*, Vermont, Healing Arts Press, 2006

Chapter 7

(1) Huffington Post, (Issue 60, Huffington, 8/2/13).

Thomas Moore, *The Dark Night of the Soul: A Guide to Finding Your Way Through Life's Ordeals*, USA, Gotham Books, Penguin Group, 2005

Marc David, *Nourishing Wisdom*, New York, Bell Tower, harmony Books, 1991

Pia Chodrun, *Comfortable With Uncertainty: 108 Teachings on Cultivating Fearlessness and Compassion*, Boston, Shambhala Publications, 2003

Marianne Williamson, *A Course in Weightloss: 21 Spiritual Lessons For Surrendering Your Weight Forever*, USA, Hay House, 2010

ACKNOWLEDGMENTS

This dream of mine would never have become a reality without Beth Sandri. Meeting her and hearing her story inspired me to put mine to better use than the one it was having stuck in my head. Beth has coached me, taught me, and motivated me to dig deep. Her wisdom and intuitive insight have been an extraordinary gift and a blessing.

The team at Balboa Press has been incredibly supportive and willing to answer my smallest concerns. Nicole Osbun, David Yoder, Elizabeth D, and Staci Kern are responsible for crafting the book you now hold in your hands. I am so very grateful.

Many thanks to Nicole Wise and Beth Grossman for creating a platform for me to share my message of experience, strength and hope.

My clients are special women and men who openly share their lives and allow me to accompany them on their very private and sacred journeys. I lovingly extend my heartfelt gratitude for this privilege. They inspire me daily to be the best version of myself.

I am incredibly blessed with healers, teachers and mentors who have seen me through my metamorphosis. I hope to continue to be enveloped by your love and guided by your wisdom.

I am both blessed with and grateful for parents, sisters, brothers-in-law, and longtime friends who have been constant sources of love and support during the darkness and the light. I cherish you and hope this book offers you with a deeper understanding of my journey.

I doubt I would have dared to even believe I could write this book if not for Eddie, my husband. You have helped me see that

I can be who I need to be, ask for what I need to have and do so without fear. Eddie, you are always beside me, sometimes behind me, but never standing in my way as I have taken the stage for my second act. Thank you for your love and constant encouragement to just *be*.

Nothing I do is without forethought, inspiration, and motivation to be the best I can for my extraordinary family of daughters and sons-in-law, stepsons and daughters-in-law, and our spectacular grandchildren. It is so very wonderful to be living this big, beautiful and joyous life. I know I have been distracted this last year as I've put these words to paper. Thank you for your patience.

With love, from the depths of my very deep soul.